CIVILIZATION IS MISSING THE BUS

SOCIAL IMPACT OF THAKUR ANUKUL CHANDRA'S MOVEMENT

DR. DEBESH PATRA

In the eerie of destitution, a lone feeble voice, gasping for air and looking for hope, wondering:

- ⚜ Who took my Thakur away?

- ⚜ Who split and stole my attention?

- ⚜ Where on the way I lost my love for Thakur?

.

.

.

Some forlorn female standing apart is wondering – who is Thakur by the way?

This book is dedicated to future leaders of
Sri Sri Thakur Anukul Chandra's movement,
which will impart a different orientation to civilization.

CONTENTS

Contents

List of Illustrations (Figure & Table)

Contents

List of Boxes

PREFACE

> You won't know if you are missing something; unless of course someone points it out. Or you are conscious about it. What happens, if you are missing the consciousness? Or, consciousness is failing you?
>
> If civilization is missing something, who on earth would know?
>
> There is a war happening, because nobody could prevent it. The train met with accident, because somebody did not notice something. Losses are real; nothing could be done and humanity has been enduring these. And many more.
>
> This study brings to your notice something that you might be missing. Less we speak about civilizational loss, better. Losses are real.

The theme of this study is mix of two separate worlds; one is spiritual world and the other is material world. We will be reflecting on ideology, which in a sense belongs to spiritual world and we would bounce the ideology on the society, which very much operates in material world. Ideology is supposedly static and sacred; whereas society is always mobile and mundane. Since Sri Sri Thakur Anukul Chandra has not seen these two worlds apart from each other, we are venturing to combine these two and reflect on human life on social fabric.

This study, presenting symbiosis of two antithetical forces, is multidisciplinary. The challenge becomes more intricate as we deal with shoots of distortion in the ideology. Obvious object of the exercise is to prevent distortion to the extent it has not already sprouted. We have attempted to chalk out a reform path for the areas which are already corroded by distortionary dialectics.

We are conducting this study with passion for the ideology, and we would like to see the society a better place to live in. We do not want civilization to miss out the contributions made by the prophet of the age. We are following up the subject with academic tools of enquiry, estimation and analysis. This is a reflective, experiential and observational research in sociology and culture. The subject spills over and covers such multiple domains as socio cultural studies with respect to popular movement, mass psychology and history. Society will benefit, if the actors in social and cultural space see value in this analysis and take pains to follow the reform agenda.

We believe that Society needs Sri Sri Thakur, in as much the same way as Sri Sri Thakur needs every member of the society. This exercise is inspired by the fact that fifty five years after Sri Sri Thakur's being off the scene, there appears to be renewed interest for Sri Sri Thakur by the society. A new generation has come to active stage who believes in happening like scientific spiritualism, evolutionary growth and rejuvenation of nature. Nature abhors status quo, as every moment in nature wants to be momentous. Whether Sri Sri Thakur's movement, after fifty five years of journey without Sri Sri Thakur's physical guidance, needs a social reality appraisal? A course correction? If the answer is in affirmation, then what are those changes?

In February 2024, I completed fifty years of my discipleship of Sri Sri Thakur Anukul Chandra. Ever since the day I was initiated, I continued to remain an active follower of Sri Sri Thakur. The initial few years after initiation was spent in disciplined environment in the midst of dedicated devotees. We learnt and practiced to work for Sri Sri Thakur. We then believed that everything we did was for Sri Sri Thakur's pleasure. As if we were born for Sri Sri Thakur and Sri Sri Thakur in turn took charge of us. I observed Sri Sri Thakur's ideology as a scholar, as a practitioner and to a limited extent as a preacher. I observed societal developments unfolding, with a steadfast belief that better days would come, with Sri Sri Thakur's influence on the time and with his blessings reflected on the lives of his countless disciples, whose number was swelling. My expectations of better time, however ambiguous and presumptuous these could be, turned out to be a little misplaced. Alas, something went amiss, I said to myself. We have nevertheless to admit that strenuous efforts have been put by dedicated devotees for more than a century and those efforts have yielded outstanding outcome, which in no small measure have contributed to the growth of the movement and to the betterment of the mankind. Lot of grounds have been covered by the movement and the movement on date holds robust optimism.

This study may be useful for future researchers. They would perhaps find baffling to fathom the gap between what was to happen and what actually did happen. Sri Sri Thakur's life and play were believed to usher in beginning of an era. That beginning had enormous promises and prospects. Future researchers would attempt to assess the impact of Sri Sri Thakur's movement on the society. So much complex developments have happened during short time of half a century that, I dread, whether history can ever trace the multiple forces which shaped and drove the course of Sri Sri Thakur's movement. I am leaving behind this account of my perception for future researchers. I am a commentator who participated in the events for past half a century.

The book in your hand is a testament of time. The book narrates stories relating to a movement which is said to be the most pervasive and powerful socio cultural movement of our time. Having the potential to rescue the world, the movement is struggling with its vibrancy and vivacity to deliver its commitment, negotiating multiple streams of chaotic social order and mankind's instinct for survival and serenity, together with aspiration for peace and prosperity.

And the commitment is to infuse life and growth in everyone, igniting love and eliminating pain, leading to life of joy and togetherness.

Mumbai

15. 08. 2024

**This study is an initiative of
Institute of Indo Aryan Studies**

Website - www.srisrithakuranukulchandra.com

Mail – iias.sstac@gmail.com

Disclaimer

This study has not been sponsored by any organization.

This is a study in sociology with respect to Sri Sri Thakur Anukul Chandra's movement and its impact on the society, in the context of civilizational requirement. Research objectivity has been maintained; without prejudice against any person and any organization.

I

FRAMEWORK OF SRI SRI THAKUR ANUKUL CHANDRA'S MOVEMENT

Be alert,

and do thou follow all the sayings and commandments of thy Love-Lord with apt attitude and mind, keen attention and thoroughness, according to necessity and be habituated to it;

be blessed and make others too.

– Sri Sri Thakur Anukul Chandra

The Message, Volume 5, page 125, 3rd edition, September 2012

CHAPTER I

FRAMEWORK OF SRI SRI THAKUR ANUKUL CHANDRA'S MOVEMENT

CHAPTER ABSTRACT

Civilizations got guided and fortified by some ideology based movements at different times in history. Twentieth century witnessed one such movement, unfolding from the life and time of Sri Sri Thakur Anukul Chandra. This chapter provides a brief account of Sri Sri Thakur Anukul Chandra's ideology, movement, and the value propositions. It outlines salient features of the ideology and those of the movement. The movement did grow and delivered a framework on the basis of which humans could look up to life of possibilities, despite problems. The movement, however encountered some headwinds after the sad demise of the progenitor. Those headwinds, some originating from within, hindered the movement at societal level. In a sweeping review of the historical developments, this chapter identifies the factors which were responsible for the diversion of the movement, post the demise. The chapter dwells on the twists and turns of time, and their depressing consequences, which together conspired to weather down the movement. Chapter however ends with a positive outlook, which highlights the regenerative power of the movement on the basis of humans' propensity to survive and succeed.

As the first chapter, the chapter lays out the backdrop for other six chapters to build on. One gets to know the founding blocks of Sri Sri Thakur Anukul Chandra's movement. And also the fault lines which apparently were caused by the leaders of the movement from within. A case has been developed for initiating reforms of the movement which is the theme of chapter six. Chapter one stands out for its detailed focus on internal working mechanism of the movement, besides its leadership structure and network.

INTRODUCTION

Devotion and discipline together outline the ideological framework in spiritual world. Spiritual world is of course integrated with so called material world, as both spirit and matter, in symbiotic combination constitute life.

Devotion and discipline find their roots in the soil of ideology. Their branches and blossoms grow and take form as man (woman included) irrigates the soil by sincere, sober and cordial activities. The overall system works following the provisions of nature. Humans is an intelligent expression of nature. Devotion and discipline come as naturally to humans as hunger and thirst do. Functioning of devotion and discipline takes infinite form and shape; therefore we find innumerable varieties of views on the subject.

The ideological framework is known as a well-designed operating guideline for spiritual practice. The ideological framework generally is seen to be large enough so as not to miss any specific desirable purpose. Therefore its overall configuration appears to be complex. Ideological framework is like a field with boundary; and the field is cultivable. So people cultivate the ideology. It is a 'frame' to 'work' on. So, whenever there is a reflection on ideology, some high impact actionable points emerge.

Most part of the ideological framework in the ultimate analysis are based on laws of nature. Closer an ideology to the nature, purer is its form and intent, and more cardinal is its applicability. If a person remains on the ideological trajectory, then he or she draws support from the nature. Sri Sri Thakur Anukul Chandra's ideology provides a natural yet original ladder for living and growing. It does not compel a person to be indoctrinated to any specific conventional religion. For Sri Sri Thakur, *dharma* (धर्म) is a natural way of living, growing and enjoying, together with the surroundings. Anyone of any religious affiliation can follow the ideology of Sri Sri Thakur without forsaking one's own religion. There is no conversion here. No individual is deprived of his (or her) progressive pursuits. Each person is led on the basis of his (or her) aptitude with refinement and for unfolding the possibilities. The framework stimulates advancement with adjustment of attitude.

We all instinctively crave for God's grace. We look up to God for our wellbeing. We seek relief from pain and we long for certain achievements. God on his part is benevolent enough to grant us whatever we genuinely work for. The necessary condition however for the materialization of God's grace is adherence to the ideological tenets. God can do anything for a person only when the person is placed in and operates within the ideological framework. It is therefore significant to note that God's grace remains contingent upon the functioning within the ideological framework. Following Sri Sri Thakur's ideology is a qualifying criterion, for many higher and better things to happen in life.

Thus goes the importance of ideology. Ideology is a tested maxim delineated by the divine. Ideology is the cover that contains the microcosm of 'being' and prescribes the process of 'becoming'. It is therefore important to 'know' the ideology in its pure and elementary form; then 'practice' the ideology in life's activities. Knowing and practicing the ideology are strenuous aspects of a person's life that require submission, determination and perspiration. Ideology then becomes an integral part of life; adding better quality and higher values to life. It may be logically derived that distortion in ideology may lead to deprivation from God's grace.

Sri Sri Thakur Anukul Chandra, being the prophet of the age, came with an ideological framework which is not something amorphous, and nor is it transitory. His ideology is a well fabricated composition for integrated life. His ideological framework is a well formulated operative package of progression on lines of providence. Of course, it requires a bit of efforts to figure out the ideology in full; that much as required to put the ideology in practice. Prophet's ideology, in all ages, come with the highest level of sanctity. Sri Sri Thakur impressed upon us that the tenets of ideology are to be observed both in letter and spirit. Every bit of prophet's ideology has immense significance and usually it comes as crux and complete. Any alteration, unknowingly or whimsically, may invite damage of unremitting consequences. Prophet's ideological formulation is not amenable to any human intervention. Some intermittent dilution however happens when ideology gets the wing of movement in the society. That has to be measured and guarded against.

The ideological framework

Figuratively, the ideological frame of Sri Sri Thakur is a pedestal of life that rests on four pillars. Those are: a) self (that is, existence); b) Ideal (that is, divine manifest); c) surrounding (that is, extension of self into family and society) and d) environment (that is, the elements of nature which serve us).

It is perhaps logical to say that the above sequence follows in order of priority. So, it starts with 'I and me', the self. Sri Sri Thakur likes to refer that as 'existence'. A person's universe centers on the person's self. But that 'self' has need for affiliation. In Sri Sri Thakur's words, the being has cohesive urge. That urge wants the 'self' to build relationships with 'many'. The intense form of affinity gets expressed as love. So love is seen naturally embedded in every person. The family and surroundings are expressions of larger self.

a. Life with living Ideal at the center

A fundamental premise of the ideological framework of Sri Sri Thakur is that every person has love for a living Ideal. That ideal is the *Guru*. Sri Sri Thakur Anukul Chandra, the latest incarnate, is the *Guru*. So *Guru* is no less than the God. It perhaps is more accurate to say that the *Guru* is the God. *Guru* is the expression of God. Like God is one, unique and irreplaceable; so is *Guru*. *Guru* is special. He is not just another person. He is the supreme. The creator of the universe has appeared in the form of *Guru*. He is all powerful. He can make and can break too. In his cosmic form, he is summation of the trinity; *Brahmaa* (ब्रम्हा), *Vishnu* (विष्णु) and *Maheshwar* (महेश्वर). He is the consummation of all divine expressions which we worship as gods and goddesses. He is the source of creation. He in his benign dispensation comes as savior and the redeemer. He fulfils the need for every one and therefore, He is all fulfiller.

Sri Sri Thakur as 'living Ideal' is a cardinal concept. First; an ideal is the personified image of the ideology. Sri Sri Thakur is said to be the ideal in the sense that the ideology has taken shape and form in him. The ideology has emerged and evolved from his persona. Following him is to follow his ideology and *vice versa*. Second, he is ideal, because, he is the best one to follow. Following his steps is assured path of nobility, mobility and security. The best one to follow by all can be the God only. God incarnated in living form by the name and form of Sri Sri Thakur Anukul Chandra. He stood for life, love and lift.

This concept as narrated in the paragraph above is founded on certain level of personal faith, experimentation and realization. At some level, with the passage of time, this has been an accepted social belief. Today in social formations, it is accepted that Sri Sri Thakur is the latest incarnate, and hence he is the Ideal to follow. He therefore stands for social solidarity, unity and integrity.

b. Love for Sri Sri Thakur is the fulcrum of transformation

Relationship with *Guru*, that is, with Sri Sri Thakur, is of love and adoration. Other attributes, as lofty as devotion, discipline, concentration, tolerance for hardship, harmony, fellow feelings, all follow from the love (with him). This love for Sri Sri Thakur is very intimate and direct. The love for Sri Sri Thakur is the nectar that the soul has been searching for. All thirsts get mitigated and sublimated when a person starts falling in love with Sri Sri Thakur.

The love for Sri Sri Thakur is the alchemy that streamlines many factors in life automatically. As life blossoms with love, one starts relishing life and life become enjoyable.

Sri Sri Thakur's personality is a fountain of love. His piercing eyes soothe the heart. The pair of eyes and ray of smile overwhelm person's joy and buoy up feelings. There is exuberance of purity and perseverance. Adrenaline rushes out, gates of emotion are thrown open; one then starts flowing in the current of inundated elixir that washes away all the burdens that were hitherto pulling one down.

A closer look at the ideological framework presents a picture of the solar system, where the sun is placed at the center and the constellation of planets are orbiting the sun. The celestial bodies are held together by some force which is love in human life. And Sri Sri Thakur, the *Guru* happens to be the sun in our life. Love for Sri Sri Thakur regulates a devotee's habits and conducts. Negative emotions and impulses get subdued by the counteracting effects of love of the lord. That is how a devotee is able to maintain balance under all types of situations.

c. Destiny demystified

Man has been endowed with freewill and capacity to do things. The ability to exercise the will power and manifesting the inherent capacity are potentially immense. But the actual application remains circumscribed; being constrained by multiple factors. Man is required to deal with those constraints; which at times come as adversities. Adversities play demonic role; retard and cripple the inherent capacity. Playing the role of *Guru* and Guide, Sri Sri Thakur enables a devotee to stretch his or her capacity and also helps to overcome and mitigate the adversities. This process may come as struggle for some. Not all are fortunate have a smooth walk in life. Sri Sri Thakur however co-travels with the devotee to cross the phase of adversities. There is no way to measure if Sri Sri Thakur attenuates the load and pain of adversities. It is however believed that he shares the load of adversities as he walks alongside the devotees. There is bit of mystery in this process, as many things happen without our knowledge. Due to the complexity involved in matters related to life, devotees turn to such practices as faith, belief, prayer, offerings etc. which invokes psychological reinforcement and spiritual solace. At the time of acute crisis, it has been occasionally felt that Sri Sri Thakur comes live.

Sri Sri Thakur's ideology helps a devotee to negotiate with future, by altering the probable outcome of the past. This is a bit abstract process, as many maneuvering happen in the background. Sri Sri Thakur knows the past of each devotee and he helps the devotee to shape his or her future. Sri Sri Thakur can remake and reshape the destiny, but there is a lot of exercises involved. That is why devotion and discipline are called for. Summarily, it can be stated that Sri Sri Thakur's ideology for a devotee works like a walking stick to support and defend as well as like an umbrella to cover against sun and rain.

Destiny has two aspects for a person. The one, which remains as destiny in the backdrop, is the accumulated outcome of past actions. That aspect of destiny is like a headless nail that is stuck on the wall. It is not easy to uproot such a nail; nor is it visibly known as to how deep the nail has gone in. Sri Sri Thakur perhaps can help to pull out or dilute such a nail. There is no definite and generic prescription to deal with such blind and intricate situation. The second aspect of destiny, which everyone deals with, relates to the formation of destiny for future. The point of intervention for both past and future is action in the present. Whatever we do in the current time has the potential to shape the future and reshape the past. This is where Sri Sri Thakur plays role and that is devotee specific. Sri Sri Thakur's ideology has the power to deal with both the aspects of destiny; one which is already formed and second, which is being formed.

Figure 1 - Schematic Diagram on the Ideology of Sri Sri Thakur

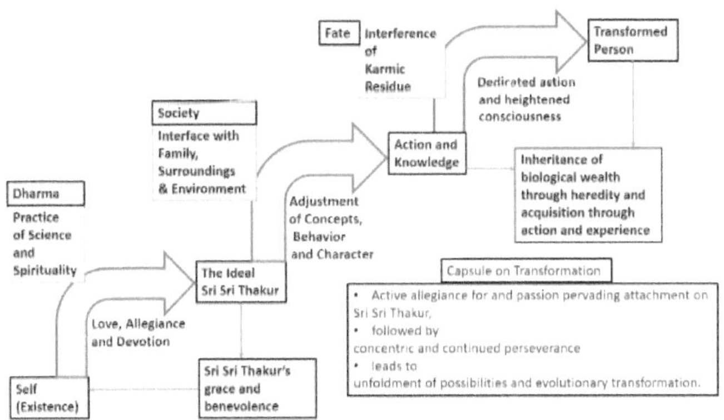

d. The ideology provides guidelines on diverse situations of life in society

Sri Sri Thakur's ideology covers such extensive subjects as humans deal with, for example: family, society, environment, aspects of collective living and growing. The ideology throws focus on issues of wide and diverse range, such as, politics, economics, diplomacy, business, health and hygiene, scientific inventions, agriculture, industries and so on. Society would do well to follow the principles of the latest prophet. The collective disorientation of many kinds may be avoided, if the prophet's views are factored in the social settings.

In Sri Sri Thakur's framework, each man and women, irrespective of one's identity and affinity, finds place of distinction. This brings out the point that while ideology deals with the forest when required; but it does in no way misses the trees. Fundamentally, the health of all trees together presents the view of the forest.

Convention and tradition play significant role in any society. While convention and tradition help to maintain the continuity of the core of culture, at times, these come in the way of adopting new ideas, particularly those which are of epoch making type. Sri Sri Thakur's ideology reflects the core of tradition and convention. But the ideology examines everything on the basis of meaning, likely consequences and scientific temper. In a sense, Sri Sri Thakur's ideology is a complete framework, which has the potential to replace the extant practices on traditional lines. That is how, the ideology is a bridge between the best from the past and innovative future. The ideology does not overthrow any convention without examining its value and usefulness. For a devotee, therefore, Sri Sri Thakur's ideology presents a filtered tradition. It is like getting to read the latest edition of a book.

Significance of Sri Sri Thakur's ideology in the context of society is that the ideology is not averse to development oriented actions like economic prosperity, technology innovation and harnessing nature without exploitation. These three factors are the leading forces in the society and their management has the ability to avert many ills of the current society. Sri Sri Thakur's ideology provides an umbrella like macro setting in the society, which makes society a conducive place to deal with lots of issues arising out of economic growth, technology refinement and usage of natural resources. The ideology deals with human being, its behavior, attitude, and outlook; all in conformity with nature and existential wellbeing. At next level, the ideology is capable to deal with the issues of state craft like polity, administration, judiciary and diplomacy. Lot of complications in the current system can be managed well and evils can be avoided, if the ideology is applied at the society level.

Box 1 - A Devotee's Monologue

(A devotee narrates in a matter of fact way)

Sri Sri Thakur, the living and moving God, is my *Guru*. I am tied with Sri Sri Thakur by the strings of love and devotion for Him. He guides me and fulfils me in the manner that is required for me. I am unique, my needs at any point in time are specific. Sri Sri Thakur knows me and my needs. He does exactly what is required for me. I owe complete allegiance to him, as a faithful follower. It is a pure unalloyed love for Sri Sri Thakur that helps me to negotiate my life, facing all the hardship, toils and troubles that I encounter. He is there with me and so I am empowered to deal with situations that emerge. I enjoy an inalienable relationship with Sri Sri Thakur. The relationship endures good time and bad time. The directions coming from him are the guidelines for me. His dicta set the path for me. My life, all my deeds and my other relationships are adjusted within this framework. This adjustment is a process of reformation and transformation for me. This process in life may be a struggle; it may not always be a cozy affair. I am alive to the fact that life may not be smooth sailing. Sri Sri Thakur remains with me in all challenging situations.

I adhere to Sri Sri Thakur's ideological tenets. So, I lead a disciplined and grateful life. The ideological framework brings meaningful practice and outcome. I usually find my inner questions answered in his literature. Sri Sri Thakur Anukul Chandra's literature comes with world of knowledge, which sets out for me what to do under various conditions. I do receive some intuitive guidance from Sri Sri Thakur. I, however, am not sure how do those intuitions origin. I usually take these as his grace. I believe that Sri Sri Thakur is gracious and bountiful.

Sri Sri Thakur is physically no more; but I feel his presence through innumerable happenings. I do believe that his ideological framework keeps him live through adherence and attachment. He comes live for his devotees. The divine power is not limited by the absence of corporeal frame. Sri Sri Thakur remains as receptive and responsive today as he was during his lifetime. It appears to me that he is all pervasive and more powerful today than earlier, as he is no more bound by laws of physiology and biology. His cosmic and contemporary care humbles me as I get overwhelmed by my feelings of gratitude.

I understand that I am weighed by my ingrained thoughts and habits. I however feel lighter and luminous as I go through the daily practices of his principles. There comes rush of energy and enthusiasm. Those keep me going.

Summarily, the ideology lays out a passage of transformation; move towards ascendency. The transformation is based on reality, and passing through strands of possibilities, it reaches actuality. One's existence and Sri Sri Thakur's ideological framework are the realities. Possibilities are immense, yet for a specific person and time, these get circumscribed by many known and unknown factors. The actualization of possibilities are function of three levers, viz, devotion (निष्ठा), attachment (आनुगत्य) and urge for action (कृति सम्बेग). These levers are tools in devotee's hands. These are hard actions; the feelings of cracking the hardness can, however, be softened by love for Sri Sri Thakur. What happens during the process, is not entirely known to devotee. But it is said that the outcome, depending on many uncertainties, could be a combination of 'magic' and 'logic'.

Table 2 - Reality, Possibility and Actuality of Transformation: Action and Outcome Matrix

		Magnified by:	Conditioned by:
Reality	1	Status of existence of self; current and accumulated past that is hidden	
	2	Prevailing surrounding conditions, including those of family	
	3	Sri Sri Thakur as *Guru* and the ideological tools	
Possibility	1	Reliance on Sri Sri Thakur and confidence arising there from (बिश्वाश ओ निर्भरता)	One's capacity and aptitude
	2	*Guru*'s direction (गुरु निर्देश ओ उसका पालन - तपस्या)	Limited view of self interest
	3	Irresistible urge to fulfill the *Guru*, may call for some sacrifice (आत्मत्याग)	Limited outlook about self and possibilities
Actuality	1	Devotion (निष्ठा)	
	2	Attachment on *Guru* (आनुगत्य)	
	3	Urge for action (कृति सम्बेग)	

It must be qualified that table 2 is sketchy, attempts to capture some actionable aspects of the ideology. It may not be exactly accurate to attempt to limit the areas of possibilities and actualities. There comes the enormity of the capacity of human being, supplemented by Sri Sri Thakur's grace. The divine possibilities have been expressed as his grace.

THE NATURE AND OBJECT OF SRI SRI THAKUR'S MOVEMENT

Sri Sri Thakur Anukul Chandra's movement had a superb course all through its journey, beginning in say, 1918, the year *Vishwa Guru Mahotsav* (विश्व गुरु महोत्सव) was celebrated at Kustiya. In that year, marked by historical developments, it was announced by some contemporary elites that the incarnate for the age has descended. It was an open invitation to larger society to come, witness and be part of the wonderful events that were being unfolded then. It was a grand spectacle of incarnation under revelation.

One can hold the view that the movement commenced since the birth of Sri Sri Thakur in September 1888. The reason for this view is that the prophet's work for materialization of his mission remains in force irrespective of the stage of his life cycle. The movement was led by no other than the prophet of the age that was Sri Sri Thakur. There was this unerring ideological framework, the time tested maxim of 'being and becoming', urge for unprecedented and innovative action, backed by the divine power and revealed knowledge. There was a band of dedicated apostles, the associates, the devotees of all genre, who, as if, were charged to alter the world order by their sheer willpower and indomitable urge to please their lord that was Sri Sri Thakur. The devotees' strength was swelling as Sri Sri Thakur's charm and grace got wings and spread over far and wide. The tools of transmission and mass mobilization were, love, service, mass recital of divine songs (कीर्तन), *satsang adhibesan* (सत्संग अधिबेशन), *utsavs* (उत्सव) and literature. *Yajan* (यजन) (self-exaltation) and *Yaajan* (याजन) (exalting others) were part of every devotee's everyday practice.

The account of Sri Sri Thakur's movement, as it was built from scratch and got spread around during Sri Sri Thakur's lifetime, has been extensively recounted and chronicled by a few devotees, who were the associates of Sri Sri Thakur. They were inspired by their *Guru* to take the ideology around for the benefit of the people. They were the real founders of Sri Sri Thakur's movement. There are thirty two books by twenty one authors, some translated, which are autobiographical in nature. The authors have primarily written these books as anecdotal accounts of their dedication for Sri Sri Thakur's mission and how they were blessed. During their lifetime, they delivered two precious values: a) love and b) liberation. These books are their contributions for the posterity. These are however mostly in Bengali language. Future researchers will find these very useful resource and reference material for presenting whole history of Sri Sri Thakur's movement. Besides these thirty volumes, there have been some more edited volumes in Bengali having collections of memories of some devotees, and life sketch of them, which also narrate the history and spirit of Sri Sri Thakur's movement. (Appendix 1)

a. Object of the movement

The movement took upon itself and shouldered very hard targets. That was to transform human being and bring about new social order that would be ideal centric and pro-evolution, taking recourse to science and spirituality. That was a tall order, and the charge was led by Sri Sri Thakur from the front. Sri Sri Thakur waged a war in favour of existence and against complexes. Existence and growth of every individual together with the surroundings and environment were all in the radar of the movement. It was a clarion call against the causes of human sufferings, may it be poverty, disease, deprivation, humiliation and retardation of any kind. These objects were mostly invisible, immeasurable and something that remained in the realm of consciousness and capability. Social manifestation of the movement was expected to be a logical corollary.

The task was to help cultivate culture in every life, family and society. That meant changes in habits, behavior, instincts, customs, convention and social order. The prevailing traditions, customs, convention were accepted and respected; but there was a clear attempt to make those meaningful and successful. A new order of seeking meaning, clarity, rinsing and renovation began at socio cultural domain. Divine leadership was seen in action for civilizational transformation. Every disciple of Sri Sri Thakur voluntarily played the role of precursor of change.

It may be strange to appreciate now that the movement was led primarily for the pleasure of Sri Sri Thakur and, secondarily, to serve his mission. When the prophet of the age was around personally, his pleasure and his desire stood supreme for the devotees. All the devotees worked with devotion, dedication and discipline for the pleasure of Sri Sri Thakur. Despite visible hardship, devotees experienced joy and jubilation in meeting his desire.

The whole humanity was in the focal range of the movement. Though it originated in the Indian subcontinent, but the thought and the script were all for the humanity. People from many countries far and wide, including advanced countries like Great Britain and United States, appreciated and encouraged the movement. Harper & Brothers publisher in New York published a Sri Sri Thakur's biography in 1962, titled 'Ocean in a Tea Cup'. Bharatiya Vidya Bhavan, Mumbai published a book, 'Answer to the Quest', Volume I in 1963 and Volume II in

1987. These publications in 1960s had appeal for the global readers and enlightened minds. A voice, echoing loud and clear in those years, was that Sri Sri Thakur's movement was out to integrate science and spirituality as well as east and west. A new light of civilization began to shine.

b. *Modus operandi* of the movement

Sri Sri Thakur Anukul Chandra's movement had no predetermined course. The design could be said to be pre-crafted. But the steering was in the grip of humankind. God respected the autonomy granted to human being. There was no command and control structure in the movement. Therefore, Sri Sri Thakur's movement is one example of auto initiated, ideal centric and wellbeing oriented mass movement. A movement where everybody puts in their life for the Ideal and Ideal brings out the best of everybody. It is not a typical movement of the type which normally whips up passion and hysteria and thrives to resist, or to fight, or to oppose, or to liberate, or for the glorification of a crusader and so on. There could be some elements of all those as mentioned; but everything in Sri Sri Thakur's movement was in conformity with the ideology, nature, cosmic energy, human values and universal fellow feelings. Sri Sri Thakur Anukul Chandra's movement is not against anybody or against any group or against any prevailing order.

So there is no inflammatory, reactive and hyperactive manifestation of this movement. Sri Sri Thakur's movement is therefore said to be an evolutionary movement, rather than revolutionary. The movement evolved out of the people's need and the movement aimed at bringing about evolution. The distinguishing feature of the movement did not thrive on such symptoms as bloodbath and mortal sacrifice of foot soldiers, incited by a cause or by a leader or by an event, or whatever. The tools of the movement were love, service, knowledge and compassion.

The movement played out at many places at the hands of many people who were unseen and unknown publicly. For example, Sri Sri Thakur personally and through his devotees, saved the lives of many people and rehabilitated many families during the post independent (post partition in 1947) riot in Bengal. Many lives were saved during World War II in Myanmar (erstwhile Burma). Many leaders were inspired and guided on one to one basis for setting the course of history. Many such events were not known publicly; least of those were documented. Those valuable developments of humanity will never be recorded in the annals of history. Such was Sri Sri Thakur's movement.

The spirit of the movement rode on undertaking basic wellbeing of people in all rounded way. Anything like social welfare, community wellbeing and social goods were not in the list of stated objectives. However, it was sure to come in phases and stages as the movement struck the roots of society.

c. Leaders in the movement

The movement gathered quite a force and got both intensive and extensive spread, when Sri Sri Thakur was active and visibly inspired his devotees. These devotees and leaders mostly operated from Satsang ashram at the center, head quartered at Himaitpur and later at Deoghar. We may call them as tier one leaders. Then there came a time, when second tier leadership got developed and they represented Sri Sri Thakur at distant places through their exemplary achievement, service and dedication. That was the expansionary phase in the movement. We can approximately fix this duration at Deoghar from 1947 to 1968. From the expansion point of view, the movement found itself on auto mode, riding on Sri Sri Thakur's manifest charm and leaders' buoyant spirit.

The leaders in those era visualized themselves that they were privileged to be tools in the hands of the prophet of the age and they worked tirelessly for apparently miraculous outcome. They worked for their *Guru*, out of love and they sacrificed their life. They were conscious of the fact that it was a rare opportunity for them to work with the prophet of the age. They were steadfast in their pursuits. Building a movement may not be in their conscious agenda. But that was when and how the seeds of the movement were sown.

The movement had no dearth of leaders in succession. At some stage it was noticed that each devotee wore two hats; one of leader and second one of follower. The common incentives were awakening and advancement. Sri Sri Thakur says, the wellbeing of your existence lies in the wellbeing of your neighbor and surroundings. That was the founding principle of leadership in Sri Sri Thakur's movement. Leadership pipeline was primed from the pool of conscious and cultivating devotees.

d. Movement after the physical demise

Sri Sri Thakur at the age of 82 left his mortal frame in January 1969. Time thereafter no more remained the same as before. The spirit of dedicated and auto initiated leadership became a rare commodity post 1969. However, the spirit did not completely die. Till date a good number of devotees are working for the movement silently. This movement was largely powered by individual drive with personal determination and dedication. The fissure in the organization did not deter individual drive. Rather it recharged those devotees who loved Sri Sri Thakur and worked for him.

After Sri Sri Thakur drew off the scene in January 1969, the movement suffered organizational split. The movement endured disunity and discord at the top leadership level. Some new organizations were created, as the three sons of Sri Sri Thakur did not get along well. Along with their separation, the movement suffered horizontal structural fracture. The top leaders exhibited signs of intolerance and for a moment, it appeared as if, Sri Sri Thakur was kept off sight.

Some devotee-leaders of bygone era got fatigued at the new developments post 1969. The movement witnessed new style of functioning by group leaders. Some new leaders saw opportunities for livelihood in the movement without much strenuous effort. The quality of the movement got diluted as it had to accommodate diverse interests, other than Sri Sri Thakur's mission. Different organized factions needed workers for diverse purposes. The dominant streams of the movement now are of different nature, serving diverse needs of different leaders. The central command of different factions appear to be inaccessible to any kind of feedback. They nevertheless remain the guardians of the movement, imbued by Sri Sri Thakur's ideology. The undercurrent of the movement continues to flow with promise. Still, there are genuine devotees, leaders and workers, working for Sri Sri Thakur's cause and putting their life at the divine feet and serving his mission.

DISTORTION DEFIES PROPHET'S MISSION

The heading about distortion may sound ironical in the first place. Didn't Sri Sri Thakur descend on this earth, amidst the humanity, to clean then prevailing distorted views of life and decadent civilizational tenor? Didn't he set in place a clean ideology? Didn't he leave behind a complete package of ideological framework with universal applicability? Was not that ideology a remarkable departure from the past, and quite a leap into the future, maintaining the eternal credo of civilizational values?

a. Genesis of the movement

Sri Sri Thakur indeed laid out a life and philosophy that was remarkable for its newness and continuity. He demonstrated every bit of his ideological elements in his life and through miraculous deeds, including the wonderful examples he set through his dedicated devotees. Flocks of devotees used to surround him at any point in time, like bees. Some amongst them dedicated their lives to work for the cause of Sri Sri Thakur. They found greater meaning in Sri Sri Thakur's mission. From their points of view, they realized the ultimate of their life in Sri Sri Thakur. Sri Sri Thakur's contemporary devotees were instruments through which the prophet was revealed and that happened through the devotees' realization and through some extraordinary experiences. Some of those have been documented in literature. Those anecdotes, numerous and strange real life experiences, amply bring out the transformation that happened to the disciples by coming in contact with Sri Sri Thakur. (Appendix 1)

Fifty five years after Sri Sri Thakur left his mortal frame, new generations of devotees constitute the bulk of the current number of disciples today. These generations of disciples grew in the ambience they lived in and they might not have got opportunity to get live touch of Sri Sri Thakur, even notionally. So the 'ideology in practice' has gone far away from 'Sri Sri Thakur, the person'.

b. Distortion happened despite safeguard

Distortion in social system may not happen overnight and may not be an episode of cataclysmic change to start with. Distortion, more often than not, always creeps in, may be from an obscure channel. Distortion takes time to surface and it still takes more time to take the shape of a resistible force. Engineered and motivated distortion might weaken the system from within, like white ants do to a wooden structure.

The spirit of society can ill afford to feign shy of incipient eruption of distortion. Distortions target the cultural substance surreptitiously and unceremoniously. Distortions also at times are launched with combative approach, ostensibly to make the deviation publicly acceptable. Fears are fostered to preempt resistance to deviation. Independent minded nonconformists are repressed, if required. Distortions are not so much a natural deterioration, though distortion may also happen due to changed conditions prevailing around. What we are witnessing today can be said to be a conspired attempt to compromise with some basic tenets of Sri Sri Thakur's ideology. It is being thrust upon unsuspecting practitioners. Of course, distortion is thriving on ignorance and attitude of indifference by the mass devotees.

Today, the size of devotees' population has grown quite large and the devotees are dispersed in all parts of the world. A large and growing base of devotees run the risk of becoming unwieldy from the point of view of maintaining discipline. But the minimum and core discipline and allegiance to the ideology can never be compromised. Sri Sri Thakur's ideological framework has been extensively depicted in the voluminous literature. It can be said that Sri Sri Thakur continues to live and speak through his literature. So far these literature have not come to center stage of social view. The irony lies in the fact that Sri Sri Thakur's ideology has so far not truly appreciated by the humanity at large. Therefore, distorted versions have a chance to paint a clean canvass.

Devotion is antidote to distortion. Devotion is caused and followed by knowledge; distortion flourishes in the pool of ignorance. Devotion brings in light and distortion invites gloom. Sri Sri Thakur dispensed devotion and discarded distortion. It is now humanity's choice.

c. Ambience resisted the ideology

Globally there appeared to be huge headwind against peaceful life during whole of twentieth century, which kept continuing till date, may be with higher intensity. There prevailed, as if, war against human existence. Any new and path breaking ideology usually meets with resistance to the point of extinction. In retrospect, we may hold the view that Sri Sri Thakur launched his ideology in the most befitting manner for the age. He got the ideology well demonstrated. It was a complete ideology; was well delivered for the humanity. The ideology got entrenched in certain quarters of society. Sri Sri Thakur did not leave any stone unturned to ensure that he bequeathed a complete package of ideology that was distinctly unique, yet not totally dissimilar from the core ideologies of the yore. Existentialism and humanism were glorified by profusion of love and compassion. The divine and eternal part of conventional culture was maintained; the discrete part of conventional culture was customized for the age. There were symphony of apparently dialectical streams like science and spirituality; household life with active detachment; predetermination and freewill. This kind of spectacularly appropriate ideology for the age is yet to receive as much reception as it deserves. Mankind is yet to appreciate the loss it has endured for not acquiescing with Sri Sri Thakur's ideology. More on this is has been dealt in Appendix 3.

After Sri Sri Thakur's said demise, evil came riding on personal aspiration of some leaders for dominating the movement. It was perhaps the play of ego and self-importance, which made the leadership to create divisions in the movement. The structure of the movement got divided on lines of affiliation to the top leaders. The developments leading to divisions and discord in the organizational set up, so wildly unfolded in the post demise period, was something that we failed to comprehend. In retrospect, we have to satisfy ourselves by attributing the division to personal aspiration and intolerance for dissent at the top leadership level. Different sections of the movement adopted and promoted different versions of ideology. Devotees at large remained submissive to the dominant leaders. Large sections of the devotees remained indifferent to the vicissitudes of the movement.

A movement that promised age of renaissance was torpedoed from within. Unfortunately, civilization appears to be drifting towards existential crisis as manifest in loss of values like trust and compassion. Annihilating threats coming from cyber space, climate change and geopolitical tensions are showing no sign of abatement. Standing on the brink of moral collapse, realizing the breakdown of convention, humanity now has started to look for something eternal and yet rational and find hope in Sri Sri Thakur.

d. Movement was attempted a hijack

For quite some time, ever since the physical withdrawal of Sri Sri Thakur in 1969, a deliberate exercise has been driven by some section of Sri Sri Thakur's devotees to counter the ideological framework that Sri Sri Thakur set up and bequeathed for the humanity. This appears to be quite uncharitable, insidious, and almost unbelievable; yet it has been so much palpable and for the damage it inflicts on the movement, this has to be spelt out and to be reckoned with. Given the fact that the negative forces emanated from influential powers that ruled within the core group of Sri Sri Thakur's affiliates, those distortions appeared to have swayed over the public. More than ideological issues, there are some commercial, legal and organizational issues involved in this. Chapter II reflects more of this.

e. Deviation trend

The ideological framework entails multipronged psychological, physical and spiritual engagements at personal level. These engagements are interlinked and constitute the actionable parameters in the framework. Any slack, alteration and low severity in action with respect to any of these variables cause suboptimal level of outcome. There has to be absolute purity and clarity on key parameters like the 'guide' and the 'self' as to who they are and the relationships between the two. Fundamental questions need clear resolution at individual level. For example, Sri Sri Thakur is the guide. A disciple's relationship with him is nonnegotiable, as there is no replacement to him. He is the object of meditation and submission. What he does and how he responds to our prayers become a divine dispensation. No one else other than Sri Sri Thakur would have the capacity to come at the place of guide. The guidelines and principles, some of which constitute core of saadhanaa, (साधना) carry sanctity and sublimity. These guidelines come by way of some mantra (मंत्र), or some daily rituals, or some offerings and so on so forth. These can never be altered under any circumstances.

To the extent, these remain within the realm of practice and process at individual level, there always remains question of seriousness, sincerity and sensitivity. But if the fundamentals are knowingly tempered by some organized force, then the ideological framework starts getting vitiated. Then there is no way that the movement would deliver the desired result. The evil takes over. That becomes a state of deviation and distortion. So distortion often happens as outcome of deliberate manipulation of system. Innocent disciples may fall victim to the engineered manipulation. Ignorance and passivism could be the fault of innocent disciples.

The cause of such deviation at societal level could also be ignorance at individual level. When large portion of humanity remain dipped in conventional practices which, more of often than not, carry huge baggage of the past, then there won't be the fresh light as Sri Sri Thakur's scientific spiritualism wants to usher in. This however may not be a desperate situation as long as Sri Sri Thakur's mission and movement remain live, active and the quest for super consciousness continues to be pursued by humanity.

Second cause of deviation emanated from engineered manipulation attempted by sections of devotees, mostly at leadership levels. This remained a societal and organizational affairs that polluted the ideology through public swaying. Following are being infused into the public mind, by an organization, which is spearheading the movement. These appear to have all the trappings of pseudo-ideologies, which are being thrust upon the gullible mass.

- ⚹ Someone was designated as *Aachaarya* (आचार्य) who apparently succeeded Sri Sri Thakur, as spiritual head. This succession of *Aachaaryas* (आचार्य) is being touted as a tradition which is claimed to have approval of Sri Sri Thakur.

- ⚹ Multiple pictures of *Aachaaryas* (आचार्य) linage are placed on same pedestal with the picture of Sri Sri Thakur in places of worship and in public congregations.

- ⚹ A different *istabhrity* (इष्टभृति) mantra has been popularized, replacing the original mantra ordained by Sri Sri Thakur.

- ⚹ The daily congregational prayer has been selectively shortened.

- ⚹ Sri Sri Thakur's original literature has also been selectively edited to suit certain purposes.

Summarily, the role and position of Sri Sri Thakur was attempted to be compromised in the mass psychology. Mass devotee was prompted to believe that Sri Sri Thakur was no more and his seat was now being adorned by his nominated successor. Perhaps, to validate and perpetuate this shift, some core principles of *saadhanaa* (साधना) were diluted.

In the miasma of cult culture, devotee's submissive and faithful sentiments were played on; Sri Sri Thakur's divinity was capitalized, organizational powers were leveraged, resources were used to promote personality cult in the name of culture. Sri Sri Thakur's popularity was symbolically used to serve narrow material interests like making money, earning reputation, wielding power and so on. Organizational outfits, publicity, regimented mandates were used for the above purposes.

OPPORTUNITIES LOST WHEN DISTORTION CREPED IN

Distortions in these core areas slowly resulted in dilution of the spirit and strength of the movement. When these deviations were introduced, Sri Sri Thakur was physically no more. The mass devotees were confused to observe that there were conflicts on material grounds at the high leadership level. The focus of the movement got diverted to managing the groups, casting aspersions, spreading canards etc. The spiritual and ideological aspects were compromised. The mass mind went astray from the path of purity and propitious perseverance. Capricious complexes got room to play.

We have painfully observed the unfortunate sliding for sufficiently longtime. Today we are witness to the dreaded phase of plunge in Sri Sri Thakur's movement. The uniqueness of Sri Sri Thakur as the incarnate and his position as the *Guru* is manifestly diluted when we observe portraits of a pantheon of progeny on the same pedestal. The pristine glory of Sri Sri Thakur's mission of 'man making' is perhaps getting converted into 'money making' in practice. The depth and dastardliness of the precipitation can hardly be assessed. Someday somebody will make a study of the disastrous fall out of these. But that would not save the movement. That would only be testimony of a civilizational suicide.

OUTLOOK FOR THE MOVEMENT – MIX OF POSITIVES AND NEGATIVES

In the complex society of our time, the movement can still avert the momentous disaster if some likeminded devotees and lovers of Sri Sri Thakur attempt to resist the slide. Attempts were made by sensible groups in various formations in many ways in the past. Those attempts took the form of power game and that set in sulking act of competitive combat. This created further divisions. The solidarity in the mass devotees are now thing of the past. Now there are many groups in the movement. What may happen in future is that amongst the mass of devotes, more splinter groups would be formed with different identities and motives. But would that be of Sri Sri Thakur's liking? Would people in general get the spiritual benefit? Would it happen by design or it would be random outcome of multiple forces working at cross purposes?

Sri Sri Thakur's movement is known for its promise to usher a new era, as generally believed by the devotees. And to a large extent, it presupposes that devotees would put their life at the altar for this to happen as collective mission. It is therefore imperative for the leaders of the movement to keep the object of the movement live and work the way its founding leaders worked with dedication.

Today the devotees of Sri Sri Thakur are not seen to be united. It is definitely a retrograde status, as Sri Sri Thakur wanted to see unified brotherhood. The strength of unity appears to have eluded the movement. The movement no longer presents sense of societal solutions and existential optimism. A somewhat silver lining that are still lurking is that the movement has kept itself out of the monolithic organizational regimentation. The movement is not dictated by any single organization; nor by someone like a 'supreme authority'. No single organization or position exercises binding regulation on the devotees so as to restrict their thought and move and enforce unquestioning obedience. This by implication permits freedom of following Sri Sri Thakur's ideology as the devotees would like to do. Accepting the fact that the movement is not united under any formal command, the movement has not allowed religious imperialism. The movement has space for all diversities and all views. The only voice that moves all the devotees into huddle voluntarily is Sri Sri Thakur's call. The credit for keeping the movement free from chain largely goes to some staunch devotees of Sri

Sri Thakur who showed uncompromising adherence to Sri Sri Thakur's ideology; notwithstanding personal hardship and adversity. These groups of devotees, currently affiliated to different camps, may shed their individualistic and reclusive stance and get reunited for the Master; as a price for their love for the Lord.

CHAPTER SUMMARY

Do we have to believe that mankind invites its own misfortune? And it repeats this again and again? No; we certainly would beg to differ from this self-inflicting hypotheses. Sri Sri Thakur came with an all fulfilling ideology, demonstrated the application of ideology in life, family and society. The Ideal (Sri Sri Thakur) and the ideology together present promise of transformation that involves understanding, adjustment in habits and behavior and adopting certain laws of science and spirituality. The ideology has been well documented and some of the literature is now available in major languages. As on date, the Ideal and ideology remain less appreciated and still lesser adopted in practice. Some kind of vicious combination of apathy and conspiracy succeeded injecting elements of pseudo ideology and attempted to camouflage the Ideal; though not hundred percent. This study is expected to bring out the reality as to what went wrong and what damage it caused to the humanity. We believe this cultural pollution is at the stage of inception. Collective conscience and wisdom would prevent the onset of total eclipse.

II

TRAILING THE MOVEMENT

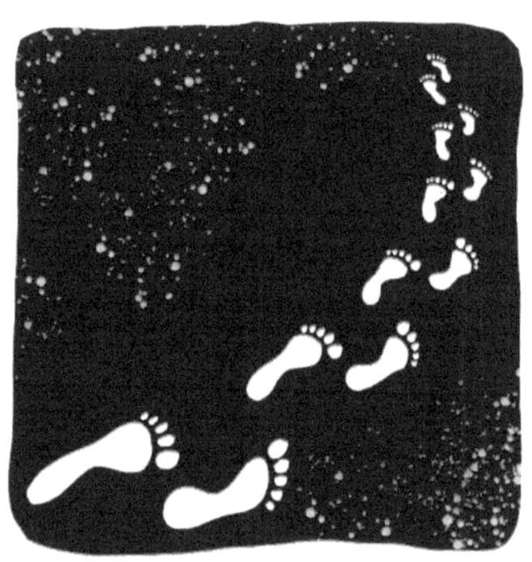

To do anything with concentric conscientious determination, thorough accuracy, all-round efficiency, and rational steps for the uphold of existence, is the essence of prayer;

blessings comes forth through it with breezy blitz,

good effulges and God smiles.

– Sri Sri Thakur Anukul Chandra

The Message, Volume 2, page 226-227, 3rd edition, January 1993

CHAPTER II

TRAILING THE MOVEMENT

CHAPTER ABSTRACT

This chapter makes microscopic observations on Sri Sri Thakur's movement, reflecting on its social impacts. The observations are based on symptoms that are visible on the ground. One, the movement has high energy at small group level; but that energy is observed to be dissipated at collective level. The movement overall gives an impression of having run into a state of disarray. Second, the movement which is high and frenzied on spiritual quotient is found low and enervated on social front. The observation is based on society's response to the movement and society's benefit from the movement. Third, a movement that lays loaded emphasis on individual role and individual's duty towards the surroundings is found lackadaisical in taking care of surrounding at the totality level. In a diagnostic trail, the chapter finds leadership disillusionment and organizational distraction as the cause and consequence of the imbalanced movement.

This chapter brings in a framework in Appendix 2 to assess social impact of the movement and goes on to find reason of its depressed state of affairs. The movement encountered a turbulence caused by a hijacking attempt, as it were, after the demise of Sri Sri Thakur. The chapter at the end reflects on corrective and curative measures. The chapter straightens the principles to be adhered to when the living ideal and progenitor of the movement goes to unseen state. The second chapter has built the core of the thesis on which subsequent five chapters would be diving deeper.

CIVILIZATIONAL TRANSFORMATION

Civilization has been vitalized by human being's quest for long, secured and enjoyable life. Human being has gone through different conditions at different times, in widely spread out geographies, going by recorded history of current and past civilizations. Overall, it can be said that the journey of human civilization has been a march towards improvement of living condition and better experience. However, there are also records of clash of civilizations and ruins of civilizations. There have been exchanges among civilizations too. So civilization presents a chequered saga of oscillated movement.

The basic units of civilization is man (woman included) and the tenure and quality of his life. The fundamental nature of that unit is to live, to grow and to enjoy. Man has been striving for those basic purposes almost instinctively, of course in many and varied ways. The civilization that we are living in for past hundred years, can be said to be a global civilization, marked by intimate communication, fast exchange and improving living conditions. Of course, there are different cultures, varied social norms, different religious practices and unequal opportunities. Here comes the prophet who works at the foundation levels and for basic needs of man. And through that, the contemporary prophet imparts progressive impulse to the civilization. Prophet comes for the whole mankind, cutting across all differences with regard to culture, religion, geography, political order and so on.

Sri Sri Thakur Anukul Chandra touches man as the basic unit of transformation. Needs of 'being' and 'becoming' of man was his concern. His ideology is designed to take care of the fundamental urge of man in a manner of universal applicability. Three corollaries follow from the above. One is that the contemporary prophet comes as world teacher. He fulfils all persons, irrespective of their differences. Humanity needs to know him and adopt the ideology, as that is the most appropriate and updated one for the present time. Second, civilizational transformation takes place through individual transformation; though there are cultural, social and political aspects involved. Third, there would remain heterogeneity in the world, amongst groups, and each specific variety in its own way contribute to the richness of the civilization.

SRI SRI THAKUR'S INTEGRATED IDEOLOGY

It is hard to distinguish between that part of ideology which deals with man as an individual (woman included) and the other part of ideology that deals with society. This is a notable feature of Sri Sri Thakur's ideology that deals with man as a social being and also as an active agent of nature. Secondly, the way ideology interacts with man is as dynamic as society, and society is known for changing with civilizational flows like scientific invention, communication, maturity of social institutions and generational changes etc. Third outstanding feature of Sri Sri Thakur's ideology is that it is as integrated as the human being, who is a seamless composite entity of body, mind, soul and society. And the fourth feature is that the mechanism of transformation that happens in human being is a self-reinforcing and iterative one; kind of a concentric virtuous cycle spiraling up, practice of that mechanism is done every day. Life with Sri Sri Thakur is a rolling process towards ascendance. Stimulated consciousness prods heightened activities, which enables to raise the status of life to the next level. And the process goes on.

It is a multistage cumulative process of transformation, as has been attempted to capture in the figure 3. Sri Sri Thakur puts in many values to the life of a person; which can be clubbed as: a) concept clarity, b) support, and c) guidance. (Column 1) These are soft and unobtrusive boosters to a devotee. Remarkable differences in thought and action do take place when we get to know the true meaning of many concepts. The idea and application of culture come lively after true meaning of concepts get revealed.

Each factor (blocks in column 1) is a powerful and transformative input for building personality. These inputs coming from Sri Sri Thakur, at some stage, work and do manifest by way of acquired personality assets. (Column 2) Clustered in three groups, some feature enriched behavior and vision, some do reflect strengthened mental framework and nobility and yet there are features displaying improved capability and productivity. (Blocks in column 2)

When a devotee's capabilities, views and output become intense and overpowering, mixed with Sri Sri Thakur's protections from evils, then the personality grows and glows. Devotee gets endowed with attributes of superior personality. (Column 3) With every progress and acquisition, there is a phase of reinforcement of those factors with which the devotee commenced his or her journey with Sri Sri Thakur. (Column 4)

There are external and unknown factors that intrude at every stage. (Bottom ribbon, touching column 1 to 3) Those can be favourable and hindering factors, on which humans have little control. Human being has to deal with those external factors. Circumstances and situations coming from these gateways could be strange, overpowering, numerous and can be life threatening as well. These factors too remain well within Sri Sri Thakur's ideological paradigm. Here Sri Sri Thakur plays gatekeeper's role.

When concepts are clear, a worldview emerges by way of operating principles. Application part of principles is important as application impacts life and creates outcome. Principles protect, provide and promote life. Principles come to us by way of process also. Process takes us through mechanisms, procedures, operating guidelines which together help us to lead life.

Figure 3 - Circularity of Multistage Acquisition and Transformation – Iterative Process

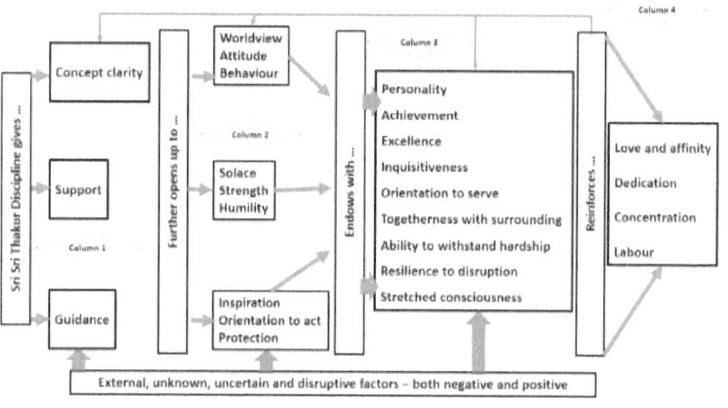

DICHOTOMY BETWEEN INDIVIDUAL LEVEL AND GROUP LEVEL

From a sociological perspective, the devotees of Sri Sri Thakur as a whole appear to be a disoriented lot today, with honorable exceptions of course. This rather disparaging observation is outcome of the multipolar direction of the movement and disillusionment prevailing at leadership level. Each devotee of Sri Sri Thakur, personal distinctiveness notwithstanding, stands testimony to a storehouse of energy and inspiration. Each devotee is conscious of his or her enlightened status for their affiliation to the prophet of the age. Small groups of devotees are generally seen to remain quite coherent and active. They know the value of purity, patience and perseverance, as the virtues propounded by their *Guru*. That presents a scene of distributed energy and high degree of social cohesion. There are quite a good number of wise and learned leaders in the movement, who are seen to be engaged in educating and inspiring the mass.

At overall level however, the performance of the large groups in the movement, appears to be lower than expected. One view is that the movement has lost its steam, sheen and promise of yesteryears. Another view is that the movement has become inward looking, rather than wider and forward looking. Yet another view, as we hear, is that the movement has taken to a slow lane before rejuvenating itself by a seer type leader, who is being awaited.

Performance assessment at overall level of groups representing Sri Sri Thakur's movement is expected to be done against two trends: a) Needs in the emerging society, and b) Sri Sri Thakur's vision and mission. The overall performance of Sri Sri Thakur's movement, as we analyze fifty five years after Sri Sri Thakur went off the scene, is not very much salutary. On a scale of one to ten, we would painfully put the marks on 4.2. (Appendix 2)

SOCIALLY DILUTED IMPACT

A reason contributing to this dismal observation is that there doesn't seem to be good social impact of the movement, except the efforts being made to spread the message of Sri Sri Thakur around. Attempt to vigorously deliver the message of Sri Sri Thakur presupposes that once a person gets to know about Sri Sri Thakur, he would follow the ideology and be a self-propelled devotee. Movement of course continually takes some mobilization measures to keep people spiritually energized. These measures are mostly by way of organizing gatherings, *satsang adhibesans* (सत्संग अधिबेशन), *utsavs* (उत्सव), celebrations and building centers and temples. Beyond these event based engagements and discourses, we hardly see visible constructive, service oriented, capacity building and philanthropic activities happening in the movement so as to make impact on the society.

It is of course a different issue, which finds sections of devotees averse to any social and philanthropic activities on the ground that these partial services don't provide complete solution to people. They hold the view that only service that can genuinely help a person is to connect the person with the *Guru*. That is spiritual service; gift of connecting with God. We are not getting into judging those viewpoints. There are different perceptions to such proposal. This study holds the view that visible and effective social welfare measures like helping communities for better education, public health, sanitary measures, and providing income generating provisions of trade and commerce are real services for life and livelihood. Of course all these require pure spirit and serviceable attitude and these are required to be provided with holistic provision of wellbeing.

The one sided view about welfare activities and absence of socially and economically relevant initiatives are symptoms of below par quality of leadership and their indifference to social issues. This situation of leadership has arisen due to fact that the movement no more attracts talented leaders. It must be qualified here that leadership in Sri Sri Thakur's movement calls for qualities like higher consciousness and divine commitment. Leaders in movement like this remain on different scale of need fulfilment and such scale usually don't fit into the standard scale that applies in society. The qualities that are valued in the society may not be those that are required in Sri Sri Thakur's movement. So a celebrated leader in the society may not find high effectiveness in Sri Sri Thakur's movement. And vice versa also may hold good. People with leadership qualities, who are high on divinity and also effective in society, are very rare. Second, the fact that effective leadership is not growing from within speaks that leadership nourishing culture is not being maintained in the movement. Movement is having paternalistic high altitude leadership, who do not seem to be open minded and accessible. Thirdly, the movement has not created that kind of avenues where talented people would be attracted for their fulfilment. More reflection on leadership in Sri Sri Thakur's movement is available in Chapter I and VI.

A salient trend of the movement has been a drastic fall in the standards of practices of core principles, impinging on quality of life and progress in spiritual realization by average disciples. The central purpose of Sri Sri Thakur's movement is to put a practitioner on auto elevator towards finer sensibilities and acquired achievements. All these require focused attention on devotion, discipline, dedication and regulated lifestyle. Sri Sri Thakur has provided some principles which are to be cultivated every day. Besides self-motivated practice, and family induced culture, social and surrounding milieu do help devotees for observing those principles. Institutional platforms, if available, supplement a person's self-practice. The current movement appears to be going slow on the self-regulation and self-development part. The movement is now on enrolment and expansion mode and, in the process, quality and austerity have become casualties.

Sri Sri Thakur's physical withdrawal — an unmitigated disruption

Loss of direction and change of purpose gripped the movement after 1969. The obvious reason which caused these two social problems was the void created by Sri Sri Thakur's withdrawal from the earth. That was a truly unsettling moment. That became worse for the devotees at large because of the confusion at the top leadership level. The change caused due to Sri Sri Thakur's physical withdrawal was not well managed for the devotees. Devotees at large were shocked in the first place, as the living ideal suddenly turned into the unseen God. Secondly, the devotees found themselves bombarded with some makeshift theories, which they could neither accept nor reject. It was indeed a trying time for the devotees as they found no settled ground, which could have accommodated ideological continuity while admitting Sri Sri Thakur's physical absence. Of course, the ideology triumphed in the long term; the devotees turned to Sri Sri Thakur's literature and found enough guidance to continue their journey of devotion while maintaining connectivity with Sri Sri Thakur.

Post 1969 was a period of shake up. For some, their faith on Sri Sri Thakur and the wrangling in the movement were irreconcilable. Many weak strings of devotion got snapped during this time. The movement's ability to hold people together, given that there were multiple warring factions, invited a mortal blow on the movement. Devotees from the lifetime of Sri Sri Thakur, the surviving contemporaries, started deserting Deoghar ashram, which was the head quarter of the movement. Sri Sri Thakur lived at Deoghar since 1946, after migrating from Himaitpur in Pabna. It appeared a period of atrophy started.

During period 1969 to 1987, there were developments which ensued emergence of new mosaic of ideological frameworks in the movement. That period witnessed emergence of many personalities, who took up leading positions and formed different groups and organizations. There were others who disputed some ideological positions of some leaders. There were personality clashes; fight for power and hegemony and so on. Tier two and tier three leaders found alignments with some organization or other. Some legal issues were fought in the courts. It was unfortunate for the human race that a movement of life and growth, which promised a new horizon, philosophy and world order, ran into rough weather. Humanity unconsciously witnessed occasion of missing opportunity.

CONVERGENCE ON IDEOLOGY IS THE NEED OF THE HOUR

The multiple groups in the movement espouse Sri Sri Thakur's various versions of ideology. Now these groups and their espousal, working at cross purposes, are making the overall movement weaker. The existence of multiple groups and even new groups getting added to the existing ones are to be taken as natural organizational and social behavior of the movement. Ideological variation among groups however is a reality that must be avoided at any cost. Devotees of Sri Sri Thakur must converge at the unalloyed ideology of Sri Sri Thakur. The following salient features may be adhered to both in letter and spirit universally.

- ⚹ Sri Sri Thakur is the *Guru*; He is the *Aachaarya* (आचार्य) and commands supreme obedience. His position can never be compromised by putting the family members on the same pedestal.

- ⚹ The process of *diksha* (दीक्षा), *istabhrity* (इष्टभृति) and meditation are to be strictly as per Sri Sri Thakur's instruction. No trace of deviation can be permitted from what Sri Sri Thakur ordained on core principles. Deviation of any type would amount to pollution in principles.

- ⚹ All group leaders must eschew bickering other groups. Multiple groups may exist and operate on the basis of affinity of members to that group; or may be on geographical basis. All the groups must pledge common goal that is to 'serve His interest and protect His image'.

- ⚹ Ultimate interest of all the groups are to serve His cause. All groups hold allegiance to Sri Sri Thakur. They are rooted in Sri Sri Thakur's culture. The ill feelings amongst them must be buried under the ground. The groups may form a confederation, or a convention forum, which will be a 'unified platform of all the groups.

- Restore steadfast adherence to Sri Sri Thakur's principles in practice. Encourage all devotees to practice the principles without fail. Create practice and demonstration centers all over the world. Make such centers and activities in the centers attractive and effective.

- Avoid promoting personality cult. Glorification of individuals should be on the basis of his or her work. Self-esteem of all leaders is important, as long as the leaders bow down before Sri Sri Thakur and follow the principles.

- All groups must be socially active, and remain active in some community welfare activities of multiple kind and scales.

- All centers and temples of Sri Sri Thakur must have well formulated engagement for visitors. These centers must be agog with socially relevant and locally feasible activities.

- Cultivate the principles of universal brotherhood, love, fellow feelings, care for nature, compassion for old and disabled, jubilation for children and so on.

AREAS OF FOCUSED ACTION

Deep functional expertise have to be developed within the movement to address the national and global issues. Sri Sri Thakur's movement aims to cover the whole humanity and it is meant to address the issues at the root. The emerging movement of Sri Sri Thakur has to focus on such issues which are complex and have far reaching implications. There are issues related to public health, environment, climate, genetics, biodiversity, and so many. Culture and social practices are fast changing, as people are adapting to new challenges. People are looking for guidance, solution, pathways, alternatives, and above all credible solace. Sri Sri Thakur's movement encompasses all issues that people are finding challenging. The movement has to keep itself relevant to the society while demonstrating Sri Sri Thakur Anukul Chandra's schemes and solutions.

Sri Sri Thakur has outlined multiple things to be done as organized initiatives. Some of those came out while he held dialogues with leaders and devotees, which are recorded in volumes of *Alochanaa Prasange* (आलोचना प्रसंगे - 23 volumes in Bengali). Those are precious actionable ideas, projects and schemes. Those must not be allowed to be lost. Action of course lies at different levels and by different persons, agencies, groups and may be by governments. The leaders of Sri Sri Thakur's movement, irrespective of their organizational affiliations and positions, are aware of those. It is just that, either focus is missing, or capacities to implement those are inadequate and resources are not available. It is admitted that organized capacity and organizational resources are always less than required for the projects to be executed. There is a need to enhance the capacity, pool the resources and take help from external agencies. It is a matter of detail who would do what and when. As far as societal needs are concerned and for the movement to be on its course, fertile and innovative minds must be put together.

Above everything else, the movement has to keep cultivating the culture. The movement has to be focused on culture as propounded by Sri Sri Thakur. What is therefore of great significance is that there would not be any scope for distortion at ideology level. Culture is a multilayer abstraction in practice to fulfil the qualitative living requirement. Sri Sri Thakur's ideological framework provides the best tool to cultivate the culture. Sri Sri Thakur's life was spent in enabling people to cultivate culture. Those effects must not be allowed to be diluted. More richness and higher values are to be added on the legacy of Sri Sri Thakur. That will be a sign of progressive movement.

DISUNITY IS NOT A PERMANENT FEATURE

The crack in unity in the movement has long history which predates 1969. But we will not get into those chronicles, as these would perhaps wreck up too much of details. Further cracks in the Sri Si Thakur's movement began within first five years of Sri Sri Thakur's sad demise in 1969. We will desist from attempting to fix singular responsibility for the division in the movement; as we know that multiple known and unknown factors played dubious roles to undercut the movement from inside and outside. Those were days of complex developments, with interpersonal issues deeply involved. We will however like to discuss the structural issues involved and will identify the validity of those issues from the ideological perspective. Those developments have bearing on assessing the social impact of Sri Sri Thakur's movement.

Sri Sri Thakur was survived by three sons. Each of them occupy venerable public position. It is unfortunate that these three brothers did not get along together after Sri Sri Thakur left his mortal frame in 1969. The eldest son, Pujyapada Amarendra Nath Chakraborty, who was actively running the administration of Satsang organization for long time, took over the whole affairs of the organization, depriving two younger brothers any supporting role. In effect, he resorted to some legal ways to take over the ownership and management of Satsang organization. If there could be one issue that made large section of devotees of that era aghast, it was this development. That action and subsequent processes driven to perpetuate that, were neither credible nor creditable. Some legal document also was used to make the eldest son the spiritual successor of Sri Sri Thakur. This was considered to be absurd and anathema, as it contravened all norms and conventions in spirituality. Some seniors among the devotees who were contemporaries of Sri Sri Thakur, led by Sri Sri Thakur's second son, Pujyapada

Vivek Ranjan Chakraborty, raised voice of revolt and repulsion.

Distortion, thus crept in, which dealt a death blow to unity amongst the devotees of Sri Sri Thakur. There was grief, disbelief and shock as hypocrisy was supposedly played on the allegiance of the older generation disciples. With heavy heart and swollen sentiment, some devotees broke away from the parent Satsang organization and looked for alternate rallying point. Few more organizations were set up as sections of devotees felt misaligned with the misdemeanor of the main Satsang organization.

At that time the second son of Sri Sri Thakur won over some principled devotees. He delved deep into Sri Sri Thakur's literature and dug out Sri Sri Thakur's directions for continuation of spiritual pursuit in the situation of sad demise of the *Guru*, the incarnate. The unalloyed principles of the movement, the ideological assets post the demise, came out to the devotees' knowledge through this process. For the second son, it was a challenge to differ from the viewpoint of the elder brother, but he did it with a view to maintain the purity and sanctity of the movement. His was a kind of lone crusade to stand against the might of the principal organization for which he had to face hardship at personal and family level. He led a stream that pledged to maintain the purity of ideology in Sri Sri Thakur's movement.

Sri Sri Thakur's third son, Pujyapada Procheta Ranjan Chakraborty, for the same reason differed from the ruling view point of main Satsang organization and formed yet another Satsang organization.

By that time and thereafter, some more small and big organizations were formed. Each of them swore in the name and ideology of Sri Sri Thakur but differed in their affiliations to some persons and some principles. Today, there are many *ashrams* or centers and temples. Despite being so many, the collective vigor is missing. Somehow there is a school of thought amongst the devotees that organizations for carrying out Sri Sri Thakur's works are necessary evils. They opine that organizations bring their own doctrines and authority structure which may run contrary to Sri Sri Thakur's principles at some time or other. They believe in doctrine of natural discipline and spontaneous unity among the like-minded devotees with common ideal and mission.

Box 2 - The ideological position in Sri Sri Thakur's movement after the physical withdrawal of *Guru*

The incarnate, the *purushottam* (पुरुषोत्तम), continues to remain the *Guru*, even when he no more remains in the mortal frame. A *ritwik* (ऋत्विक) (clergyman) imparts *dikshaa* (दीक्षा) (initiation ritual) as Sri Sri Thakur's authorized representative. The process of initiation would be the same as laid down by Sri Sri Thakur. It is to be understood that Sri Sri Thakur in unseen form imparts *diksha* (दीक्षा), of course, the *ritwik* (ऋत्विक) conducts the *dikshaa* (दीक्षा) ceremony.

The process of spiritual pursuit would remain the same as prescribed by Sri Sri Thakur. The *mantra* (मंत्र) for *istabhrity* (इष्टभृति) and *pranaam* (प्रणाम) and the process of meditation would remain the same what Sri Sri Thakur laid down.

Istabhrity (ईस्टभृति) is to be offered every day and on thirtieth day the total sum is to be presented to someone who qualifies as per criteria laid down by Sri Sri Thakur. Those criteria in sum and substance point to a devotee *par excellence*. One has to make a choice amongst the alternative devotees available. It is preferred if the devotee chosen, fulfilling the laid down criteria, also happens to be a person from Sri Sri Thakur's lineage. It is to be noted that the *istabhrity* (ईस्टभृति) is offered for Sri Sri Thakur's pleasure. *Istabhrity* (ईस्टभृति) is not to be considered a subscription to any initiative. It is a dedication with devotion for the pleasure of the Lord and through that process the surroundings and environment are also nurtured.

The ideological tenets constituting the spiritual framework ordained by Sri Sri Thakur cannot be altered by anybody. It is sacrosanct.

MIST OF MIX UP

The ultimate test of the movement lies in how much the movement enables people at large to lead progressive and balanced life, following the ideology of Sri Sri Thakur. Sri Sri Thakur served every individual for his (or her) good and growing life as per personal distinctive potential. It appears, the mass disciples of Sri Sri Thakur in the post 1969 era, are not able to distinguish on the following two fronts:

a. Satsang as an organization and Satsang as a school of devotees (community of lovers of existence)

b. Leadership by a devotee and leadership by a family member of Sri Sri Thakur

    a. Satsang vs. Satsang

There are some organizations which are 'Satsang' by name; for example Satsang Beas and Satsang Agra. The organization which spearheaded Sri Sri Thakur's activities, was registered as Satsang Pabna and then later Satsang Deoghar. People in common parlance would know that Satsang at Deoghar is the main (parent) organization, which is engaged in organizing Sri Sri Thakur Anukul Chandra's philanthropic and cultural activities. Those organizations, namely Satsang Deoghar and Satsang Pabna were offshoots of Sri Sri Thakur's human welfare related activities. Satsang, Deoghar has its own administrative structure and governing rules etc. Being the parent organization, Satsang Deoghar has large affiliates, wide networks and good resources.

There are some other organizations which are also known as Satsang and they are doing Sri Sri Thakur's ideological organizational works at Deoghar as well as at some other places. Satsang at Himaitpur, Satsang at Gidhni are examples of such organization which are similar in name, do similar work, but separate organizational entities.

Every disciple of Sri Sri Thakur is not a member of Satsang organization. Being a disciple of Sri Sri Thakur is an act of indoctrination by the ideology, which does not necessarily entail affiliation with any Satsang organization. However, it is considered to be a good practice to remain in association with people of similar faith, for the purpose of carrying out similar activities and having exchanges and camaraderie with fellow brothers-in-faith.

Sri Sri Thakur's movement is much wider in ambit and ramification than those of all the Satsang organizations put together. Sri Sri Thakur's is a movement, a collective force with spirit and structure for the whole humanity. Sri Sri Thakur's movement is much above and much broader than the streams of Satsang organizations. Satsang organizations are offshoots of Sri Sri Thakur's benign and bountiful activities. Ashrams, during Sri Sri Thakur's times, were known as 'man making factories'.

The existence of multiple organizations, unconnected to each other, is a socio cultural phenomenon in a society marked by diversity, heterogeneity and freedom of association. Having multiple organizations for a similar cause in a movement is not much of a problem. What is of significance is their operating behavior and interrelationship among them.

Satsangee (सतसंगी) is a person who remains on the path of existential propitious living. Being a *Satsangee* (सतसंगी) is something to deal with a person's attitude and lifestyle. His or her life remains on progressive trajectory, having been rooted in the wellbeing of existence. He (or she) need not be a disciple of Sri Sri Thakur. Nor he (or she) is required to be formally affiliated to any organization having Satsang in the name. But being a disciple and following the principles ensure progressive living and existential proliferation.

Satsang as a concept means association of devoted people. Satsang as verb means being in and associating with the company of devotees. This requires one to remain in state of concentration with inspiration for higher consciousness and virtuous action.

b. Leadership by birth and by culture

Sri Sri Thakur's movement historically has witnessed leadership streams arising from two stocks. One stock is from the leading devotees and the other arising from the progeny of Sri Sri Thakur. Leaders by heredity is natural in a movement where the progenitor (the Ideal) led a family life and has members from his illustrious family line.

In an ideal situation, both the streams could work in unison, playing their respective functional role and complementing the role of others. But human beings, particularly at the summit level, are generally seen to be ambitious and intolerant of counterparts; of course there are notable exceptions. People with different aptitude and aspiration may have separate way of functioning. Then there arises conflict and each stream would form their own compatible coterie and split from other group. Exactly the same dynamics played out in Sri Sri Thakur's movement. Everybody follows Sri Sri Thakur, but their leadership style differs and their organizational outfits are different. So here different groups have been formed and they are found to be having clash of opinion with each other. All the groups swear by the ideology of Sri Sri Thakur, but in actuality the leadership works to maintain their group identity, justifying their stated differences. And this creates situation of hard choice for the devotees at large.

Going by the ideological point of view, there is hardly any difference with respect to leadership value between the streams of stock, offspring or devotees. What really matters is leader's personal qualities. But society always sees something extra with the leaders from the hereditary stock, as the heredity carries inborn possibilities. Significant test criteria to differentiate between leaders in Sri Sri Thakur's movement is the singular allegiance to Sri Sri Thakur and unblemished commitment to establish Sri Sri Thakur's ideology.

Leaders need organization structure and organization needs leaders. Today, in some quarters of the movement, leadership at mass level is largely seen engaged in glorifying the super leaders, who are occupying top position in some organizations being the eldest member of the Sri Sri Thakur's family lineage. A rational approach tells us that no individual is infallible and no one is comparable, even remotely, with Sri Sri Thakur. No one should err to find a successor to Sri Sri Thakur amongst his progeny. The incarnation of Sri Sri Thakur is a cosmic phenomenon that was triggered by a sudden mutation and no biological formulation can explain that happening. It is logical not to stretch the hereditary potential beyond the level of possibilities.

Sri Sri Thakur's progeny are undoubtedly blessed with immense inherent possibilities, which are subject to cultivation and refinement. They are human beings and souls, being endowed with genetic wealth, but not without human frailties. Illustrious members from Sri Sri Thakur's family lineage are expected to cultivate their hereditary qualities and get social platform to serve the society. Let them be evolved super leader; no one need to necessarily decorate them. More than adulation, they need devotees' appreciation.

CHAPTER SUMMARY

The catastrophe, if we are allowed to say so, of attempting to dilute the ideology of Sri Sri Thakur has not met with full success of inviting dooms day for the humanity. Sri Sri Thakur is actively guiding and guarding the human destiny. He took ample measures for the ideology to remain incorrupt, despite attempt to do so by some section of his devotees. However, people who are promoting diversion and deviation in Sri Sri Thakur's movement are sure to face the consequence of their misguided misdemeanor.

Sri Sri Thakur is supreme father and he would take care of his children. His life that evolved into mission and movement, with the ideological construct, will keep the promise of becoming and belonging for the mankind. Distortions have crept in and this study is analyzing the distortion with a view to keep the ideology pristine. Well-meaning individuals with zest for life will seek joy in Sri Sri Thakur's movement of peace, progress and prosperity. Sri Sri Thakur's movement is based on individuals' freewill and passion pervading attachment on the Lord. Human being can achieve the seemingly impossible feat by following Sri Sri Thakur's ideology in practice. Every life can experience the migration to the zone of enhanced possibility. These are the promises of Sri Sri Thakur's movement.

Box 3 - Sri Sri Thakur provides lead to civilizational progress

Sri Sri Thakur Anukul Chandra's life, conducts, philosophy and guidance, all put together qualify him as the most required leader of our time. People of various countries, religions, cultures and languages found spectacular manifestation of the 'man in need'. He was the person, the manifestation of divine, for whom humanity waited for ages. He was a man who exceeded all expectations of public by his look, appearance, energy, compassion, intelligence and vision and what not.

He came with a message for the humanity. Message was, 'hey, come to me; love me; follow my steps; you have nothing to worry about'. People chose him as friend, philosopher and guide for his unusual dealings, displaying his supernatural power, soothing behavior, ability to pierce through other's mind, provide help as prayed for, ability to see past and future of people and provide unerring indications. His ideology is combination of science and spirituality; no bias on the basis of a person's social and economic status. He had the power to impart energy to others and yet dealt everything on human plane.

Sri Sri Thakur remains equally unfazed when he is either glorified or defamed. What concerns him is when his ideology gets defied and defiled, as those actions open gateway to misery for people.

He treated everyone as man and drove each one out of limitations, bondage, sorrows and sufferings. Temporal identity factors like the conventional religion, country of birth, economic status, social background, were kept to view the person's current status, but were disregarded for future possibilities.

Eternity was in his view, yet he lived here and now. He never for a moment shied away from attempts by others to conduct rational scrutiny on him. Even doubts and suspicions cast at him were faced with notes of humble welcome. His life was an open book. Like every book carries depth of knowledge, his appearance shone with wealth of divinity underneath. He was present everywhere with his prowess to do anything. He fulfilled all the earlier prophets and he presented himself as the updated prophet of the time. Sri Sri Thakur's principles, progressive as these are, can be followed by all irrespective of one's religious affiliation by birth.

Humanity would benefit from the extraordinary power generously dispensed by Sri Sri Thakur. He had in his purview the anatomy of human system, philosophy of soul, epistemology of culture and astronomy of universe. He knew the genesis of creation, the process of preservation and the acceleration of motion.

Sri Sri Thakur stands there as world teacher. This view does not mean to be an epithet to indicate any position and superiority of Sri Sri Thakur. There is no claim to Himalayan status. It only means to suggest that anyone on this planet can benefit by following his ideology.

III

DEVOTION DEFIES DECENTRALIZED ATTENTION

He, who serves people with their individual distinctiveness and makes them well up with unbreakable inter-interested fellow-feeling and serves the Providence with every blessed untiring uphill go of life,

being glorified by adherence, allegiance and active service for the Love,

is a blessed boon to society.

– Sri Sri Thakur Anukul Chandra

The Message, Volume 3, page 107-108, 3rd edition, March 1998

CHAPTER III

DEVOTION DEFIES DECENTRALIZED ATTENTION

CHAPTER ABSTRACT

This chapter focuses issue of succession to prophet. The issue stems from the dominant contemporary narrative of the movement. Keeping in view the prevailing cacophony, the issue has been examined on the basis of principle. In continuation of the post demise ideological position stated in chapter II, this chapter reflects on the subject from the point of view of cultural purity.

INTRODUCTION

'Be concentric', says Sri Sri Thakur.

With devotion and love for Sri Sri Thakur, the devotees adhere to Sri Sri Thakur's ideology. The devotees believe that Sri Sri Thakur is God's incarnation on the earth and humanity would do well in knowing and following His ideology. Adherence to His principles is a secured path of progress, as it facilitates transformation and provides strength and support.

Concentricity centers around the Ideal and Ideal is Sri Sri Thakur Anukul Chandra. Concentricity implies single point of focus and attention; it is the zero point within a concentric circle. It means convergence of affiliations to 'one' at the center. It also means, single point of reference and unicentral attachment. Sri Sri Thakur Anukul Chandra is that image of concentration for the devotees. The devotees love Him; He loves the devotees too; this mutual attraction is the drive for concentric go. Sri Sri Thakur works for the devotees like the center of gravity holds all objects on the earth.

Sri Sri Thakur as incarnate is a unique manifestation of nature, where in godhood is seen to be revealed. He transmits the exuberance to His devotee as the devotee exhilarates in His grace. In this mutual exchange, the divine-head and the devotee share a bondage that is exclusive and inalienable.

UNIQUE FORM OF INCARNATE

The incarnate of the age played human role in the form of Sri Sri Thakur Anukul Chandra. (1888 – 1969) That is a unique image reflecting kaleidoscopic blend of humanity and divinity. That form is endowed with expressions that are unparalleled, inimitable and can hardly be bargained for substitute. The grace and gratitude that flow from His persona are akin to the rays and radiance that emit from the Sun.

Of late, a somewhat strange phenomenon has gripped Sri Sri Thakur's movement as it is visible at the mass level. Some sections of the devotees are placing a family lineage as Sri Sri Thakur's successor. They think that there has to be a living representative of Sri Sri Thakur at all time. There are others in the movement, who are opposed to the concept of one living representative of Sri Sri Thakur. For those who oppose the family lineage view, it is sacrilegious to suggest that any person of any status by birth or by acquisition, can be placed on the same pedestal as that of Sri Sri Thakur. His position as *Guru* is undisputable and therefore, there is no role holder, be it spiritual and temporal, who can claim a place at His height. All the roles and credentials that are found lofty in the spiritual world including the title like *Aachaarya* (आचार्य) find befitting applicability on Sri Sri Thakur Anukul Chandra. He alone is to be followed; His attributes are to be acquired; and His principles are to be practiced in pursuit of progress. Attempt to decorate any other person of any background, as *Aachaarya* (आचार्य), would be both misplaced and misleading.

No successor to incarnate

Sri Sri Thakur exemplified a pattern of life of a *gruhi sanyaasi* (गृही सन्यासी) (household monk), living active and progressive life in concord with the surroundings and environment. His ideological paradigm centers on ideal centric and action oriented life that strives for becoming and belonging. By way of biological relationships, Sri Sri Thakur has bequeathed linages of progeny who are generally known for their sublime spiritual heredity. Sri Sri Thakur's family trail is believed to be imbued with high spiritual quotient having immense possibilities in their respective life. Like hereditary inheritance of genealogical asset in any other family, the possibilities that Sri Sri Thakur's progeny hold out varies from person to person in that lineage. By no stretch of imagination, the incarnate's genealogical possibilities can be restricted and defined to any single pattern. At the same time, no family member is endowed with the ability to succeed Sri Sri Thakur as *Guru* or as *Aachaarya*. The physical manifestations of supreme father by way of incarnate can hardly be shared; nor can those be duplicated. And if ever any dubious attempt to usurp the position of *Guru* and *Aachaarya* and positioning the same in public mind is made, it would violate the cardinal principles of incarnate. One of the cardinal principles of incarnate is that He is sovereign and indivisible in the spiritual space of a devotee and also in the collective mind. Even after His physical demise, Sri Sri Thakur Anukul Chandra remains as the *Guru* and the *Aachaarya* (आचार्य). He alone is to be loved and His principles, as codified in His sayings, are to be followed.

TRADITION OF PURITY

A section of devotees in the movement appears to be deeply sunk in belief that Sri Sri Thakur Anukul Chandra designated his eldest son as *Pradhaan Aachaarya* (प्रधान आचार्य) (Chief *Aachaarya*). It has been seen for past few generations in that family that the eldest successor is being designated as *Pradhan Aachaarya*. They believe that *Aachaarya paramparaa* (आचार्य परंपरा) (tradition of spiritual heads in succession) enjoys a mandated position and powers of a spiritual guide. In the context of Sri Sri Thakur's movement, this is to be seen as a practice being followed for smooth succession of power in *Satsang* organization, Deoghar.

Satsang organization is feathered by devotees' love for Sri Sri Thakur. The devotees hold faithful desire that the organization is run by following the principles laid down by Sri Sri Thakur. Sri Sri Thakur has provided ideological guidelines for all aspects of life including running a spiritual organization. One such principles mandates to keep the Ideal (the founder, Sri Sri Thakur) alive and follow the principles undiluted. It is never desirable to bring duality in attention and deviate from the principles laid down by Sri Sri Thakur. Every disciple is mandated to have direct communion with Sri Sri Thakur and let Sri Sri Thakur come live for each disciple with concentric go. Let mass be mobilized with the tools of love, service and dedication, all for Sri Sri Thakur and also for others in the surroundings for the sake of Sri Sri Thakur's pleasure.

A disciple is initiated to Sri Sri Thakur on pledge. That initiation is as fundamental a connection as umbilical cord. Initiation requires one to practice all spiritual conducts as prescribed by Sri Sri Thakur; everything being act of obeisance and observance. That practice brings regulation in the life of the disciple. Dilution in the subject of devotion brings about distraction. When there is distraction at individual level, there is bound to be chaos at collective level and the social impact of Sri Sri Thakur's movement get obfuscated.

We believe that Sri Sri Thakur has not laid down any such provision as *aachaarya paramparaa* (आचार्य परंपरा). Satsang, Deoghar leadership have perhaps chosen to adopt this as a convention to nominate the organization head's succession. If it is treated as an organization's management issue, then it is to be understood that way. However that organizational convention can hardly be said to have any connection with Sri Sri Thakur's ideological paradigm. If for the sake of organizational management practices, Sri Sri Thakur's core ideological tenets are compromised, then that would amount to distortion. World needs Sri Sri Thakur's movement to spread far and wide and be strengthened for the benefit of humanity. That would not happen, if a barrage of distortions in the core spiritual practices cast their shadow on the purity and sanctity of Sri Sri Thakur's ideological package in practice. May the leadership in Sri Sri Thakur's movement do introspection and rise above self-glorification and place Sri Sri Thakur's image and interest above everything else. Sri Sri Thakur gracefully created and left behind a huge cultural asset and goodwill that should not be frittered away for the sake of personal or family glorification. Sri Sri Thakur is supreme. Humanity's quest for universal wellbeing is sublime and that is the movement's core interest. Humankind has to turn to Sri Sri Thakur for the evolution and transformation of existence and consciousness. No organizational discipline can ever be accorded priority over Sri Sri Thakur's ideological precepts.

SRI SRI THAKUR'S DESIRE

Sri Sri Thakur desired to bring the humanity under the unifying umbrella of the current incarnate. He wanted His place in devotee's heart and on social canvass to remain pure and pristine. Let everyone remain exalted with existential propitious bloom. With that as objective, may the movement relook at the organizational operating strategy and may every devotee of Sri Sri Thakur renew his or her pledge for Sri Sri Thakur. We know that Sri Sri Thakur alone is our savior and we have His ideology as the path. Let no deviation, espoused for any organizational concern, bring obstruction in humanity's quest for life and growth.

CHAPTER SUMMARY

Sri Sri Thakur is *Guru* and he is the *Aachaarya* (आचार्य) (demonstrator). He alone is the object and subject of our pursuit and perseverance. This solemn allegiance to Sri Sri Thakur is the basis of Sri Sri Thakur's ideological movement. There can be various types and grades of demonstrators in the spiritual world. But in Sri Sri Thakur's ideology which we all subscribe to, there is only one demonstrator and that is Sri Sri

Thakur. He is the living example of his ideology. He does what he says and thereby he sets the standard. The movement has to come out of any concocted version that are going round. This study has outlined a correction path, of course in the context of social impact.

IV

SPIRITUAL DEVALUATION AND SOCIAL LOSS

Be thou compassionate to the sufferer;

serve him with every considerate compassion;

thus do drive away his calamities and be blessed.

– Sri Sri Thakur Anukul Chandra

The Message, Volume 3, page 129, 3rd edition, March 1998

CHAPTER IV

SPIRITUAL DEVALUATION AND SOCIAL LOSS

CHAPTER ABSTRACT

This chapter brings exclusive focus on spiritual health of the movement. The chapter focuses on the consequences of whatever distortion that is observed in Sri Sri Thakur's movement. This is an attempt to understand the possible causes of slowdown in Sri Sri Thakur's movement, particularly with respect to society. It must be caveated that no direct and causal relationship between ideological distortion and 'loss and damage' has been established. Most of whatever has been analyzed are based on observation sharpened by rational belief.

INTRODUCTION

Distortion leads to destruction and destruction results in loss. Loss and damage in the context of ideology's impact on the society is so deceptive and delusional that it may be easier to explain that with analogy of rust corroding the iron. In the affairs of the society, ideology is an implicit factor like conscience in human system. The impact of changing ideology becomes visible in the society after a time lag. Today, after fifty five years of Sri Sri Thakur's sad demise, we not only see some impacts glaringly, we also intuitively shudder to visualize the ill impacts that the society is waiting for. We have for us lessons from history with respect to distortion that happened to the ideology of previous prophets past their tenure. Sri Sri Thakur unraveled some mysterious records of the previous prophets, post their departure. This time around, Sri Sri Thakur took *a priori* measures to ward off such elements which caused the distortion to creep in earlier. Even now, in whichever way Sri Sri Thakur works, he must be taking care to ensure that people follow the right principle and reap the benign benefits of his incarnation.

Sri Sri Thakur Anukul Chandra descended on the planet with the mission of promoting human wellbeing while banishing sufferings. Object of Sri Sri Thakur's movement is to propel Sri Sri Thakur's mission. To the extent, large section of humanity remain untouched by the movement, humanity continues to suffer, may be out of ignorance and also out of negligence.

LIFE OF ACTION, LIFE WITHOUT ANXIETY

A child remains carefree as long as she is under the watchful eyes of parents. As she grows up and gets into her world, she starts living life of her own and slowly feels the heat of life. This is natural and universal phenomenon, with subjective variation.

Sri Sri Thakur offers a solution that makes us aware that everyone remains under the protective arms of supreme father. When that supreme father remains available, accessible and communicable in human form, then everyone has the option to remain carefree to the extent one is surrendered. Sri Sri Thakur takes charge of all anxieties, sorrows and pain points. The process required is to follow Sri Sri Thakur's ideology.

Sri Sri Thakur's overarching focus as far as man's life and happiness are concerned is that every person would remain engaged with action (कर्म), disregarding hindrance, obstacles, hardship and impasses, whatever come on the way. The only qualifying condition of conducting oneself is to follow principles of virtue and law of nature, which is otherwise known as *dharma* (धर्म).

Sri Sri Thakur's movement today has the unfinished agenda to reach his message across everyone without exclusion. It is undoubtedly a tall order to reach everyone across the globe; but that is what the prophet's mission is. There are actions at various levels; at individual level, organizational level and movement level. Every disciple of Sri Sri Thakur has been enjoined with this responsibility, in the interest of collective welfare of the humanity. Till such time as large segment of humanity does not take shelter of the current prophet, the shade of anxiety will prevail like cluster of dark clouds. We perhaps will be well advised to invite sun in our life, so that darkness gets dispelled. More on this is available in Chapter VI.

SPIRITUAL DEGRADATION

The damage to society due to misdirected tenor of Sri Sri Thakur movement, as is believed to be happening for past fifty five years, can hardly be estimated. The task is considered to be as complicated as, for example, the estimation of loss and damage to the society due to decline in moral standards in the work force. Since the loss is against a potential benefit, there is no way to measure the potential benefit. However, we know that the potential outcome of Sri Sri Thakur's desired movement is immense. One unidentifiable and variable development that normally happens when Sri Sri Thakur's ideology is followed is transformation. The degree of transformation always remain in the realm of possibility and that is hardly amenable to any estimation.

Sri Sri Thakur hinted at some surprising possibilities. Some example of radical possibilities pointed out by Sri Sri Thakur are: 'The partition of undivided India (pre-1947 India) could have been avoided.' 'India will come to the position of world teacher'. These are not exact quotes; these are sense of what spectacular, seemingly strange possibilities that Sri Sri Thakur indicated. If society does not pay heed to His ideology, then those developments would not happen and nobody would know about those. He further said, 'there is life in other planets'. 'Sun inside is cold'. He could see 'atoms getting dissolved into particles'. These are certainly not facts; nor are these fantasies and fictions either. Each of these was hints provided by Sri Sri Thakur and therefore can be explored to translate those into facts and possibilities. Summarily, it can be stated that when prophet's hints and wishes are ignored, then we tend to suffer potential loss, which remain unknown and therefore incalculable. And that applies to any aspect of life and society, may be at personal level or collective level.

Sri Sri Thakur's movement therefore has enormous tasks to perform now. Leaders of the movement have responsibility to translate the possibilities hinted by Sri Sri Thakur into reality. Leaders have to take up initiatives based on hints provided by Sri Sri Thakur. Leaders have to ensure that the bliss and beatitude that Sri Sri Thakur's ideology inherently promised are indeed availed and people are benefited. Large social ecosystems conducive to cultivate Sri Sri Thakur's culture have to be created. All these of course require steadfast adherence to the principles laid down by Sri Sri Thakur. If the spirituality is not observed with purity and sincerity, then the resultant loss at individual as well as at social level will be colossal in terms of opportunities lost.

'Concentration' at personal level and 'integration' at social level are perhaps corollary to each other. Sri Sri Thakur's ideology touches the lives of people at both the levels. If there is some distortion of ideology at execution level, then it leads to disintegration at both the levels. Personality gets disintegrated and society gets disunited. These are silent developments. Even after these developments start manifesting after some incubation period, it takes time to understand as to what happened and why. Corrective action needs reforms, but that is not easy task. Life of individual and time of society are flowing entities; not possible to retrace and retract. There is only one recourse available, which is to keep ideology unalloyed. That is leadership's responsibility at society level.

Disunity in the movement is primarily caused and contributed by disinterested and disoriented individuals in the group. How much disinterest and disorientation have crept in at devotees' level is not easy to assess. Ideological focus helps to maintain the level and intensity of interest and orientation of the devotees. This happens at individual's psychology and surrounding level. Leaders in the movement need to remain guarded that ideological disorientation don't affect the individuals. It may be worth mentioning here that Sri Sri Thakur's ideology operates on people through a mechanism known as 'psycho spiritual'. At application stage, this process gets personalized through Sri Sri Thakur's guidance. A distortion in ideology creates disorder in the operating process and runs the risk of making it dysfunctional. It is therefore significant to remain alert that ideology is put to practice as per Sri Sri Thakur's laid down guideline.

COLOSSAL LOSS AND DAMAGE TO HUMANITY

Today one is seldom surprised when one comes across news of natural calamities, wars, dishonesty leading to scams, etc. happening around. Such occurrences of common danger have become so frequent that people have come to admit these as cruel play of fate, from which there does not seem to be any escape. There is stoic suffering going on at mass level. We however continue to believe that some of these could be prevented, at least partially, and human tragedy could have been lessened, if overall there were purity, honesty and sensitivity to nature and if divinity would have prevailed intensely and vigorously at all levels in the society. Sri Sri Thakur said that mass destruction arising out of natural calamities could be avoided, if we knew the triggering factors behind those occurrences. Every devotee undoubtedly is responsible for self and surroundings. And collectivity of devotees, represented by groups and organizations, certainly carry higher responsibilities for undertaking mammoth tasks of preventing mishaps, at least those which are avoidable.

The mechanism of micro behavior aggregating to a macro event is not known to everybody. It is least that anybody can control such mega and natural chain of causalities. That is why humanity perhaps attribute these to such forces as 'super natural' and 'acts of God'. It may be an interesting exercise to search real time solutions of these unknown and so far unknowable problems in Sri Sri Thakur. Sri Sri Thakur appears to be carrying inexhaustible pool of solutions to the myriads of problems that humanity is beset with. And if that is not tapped, then humanity is certainly deprived of something valuable.

Spirituality brings heighted sensitivity. That sensitivity excludes nothing and could be stretched to cover the humanity. Sri Sri Thakur's definition of spirituality encompassed all kinds of enquires. Sri Sri Thakur's movement was scientific to the core. He set up laboratories in his ashram in which talented scientists were conducting research. Today's leaders of the movement owe responsibility for carrying on the spirit of scientific research. If that kind of research has become things of the past for last fifty five years, is it not a colossal loss?

It is understood that it requires huge resource mobilization for conducting research and innovation activities. Is it only scarcity of resource that is preventing from conducting research and innovation? Or is it scarcity of ideas? Or is it dearth of leadership? Or is it lack of drive? May be bit of everything together is causing inertia. The procrastination in materializing Sri Sri Thakur's vision is costing a bomb for the humanity. Humanity is not able to reap the benefit which Sri Sri Thakur's movement is supposed to cause.

CHAPTER SUMMARY

Ideological purity sets the cultural foundation of a movement strong. Ideological elements have far reaching implications, some part implicit and some explicit. Culture has to be built based on ideology.

Sri Sri Thakur's ideological foundation is so well built that it has the capability to survive few millenniums. But the culture has to be cultivated, social norms have to be set by practice and solutions are to be found for the problems of the age. Each member of the society will feel part of Sri Sri Thakur's movement if that kind of impactful sensitization is created. Conversely and unfortunately, if the ideology is misplaced, not implemented and not demonstrated, then there will be damage and loss of far reaching consequences. This study is meant to save the humanity from the incipient loss. Society must know Sri Sri Thakur's ideology and accrue the benefits of prophet's contribution.

Today, we perhaps live at a time, when a solution of serious impact is available, but is not being accepted due to ignorance. Still worse, those who accepted it hardly are inclined to make use of it, may be due to indifference. Will this be termed as misfortune for the humanity? Do we all have a tiny bit of contributory participation in this?

V

SWOT ANALYSIS OF THE MOVEMENT

The act of binding oneself with the Ideal,

in love, worship and admiration and to live on accordingly in an acceleration of one's being and becoming

is Religion to me.

– Sri Sri Thakur Anukul Chandra

The Message, Volume 1, page 158, 6th edition, May 1987

CHAPTER V

SWOT ANALYSIS OF THE MOVEMENT

CHAPTER ABSTRACT

Sri Sri Thakur Anukul Chandra's movement is a flowing force. The movement is a confluence of ideology, society and dedicated drive of leaderships. There are factors which are amenable to intervention and there are also factors outside, which the movement negotiates with. As things stand now at the end of the previous four chapters, that Sri Sri Thakur's movement requires a renewed leadership level course correction. That requires an intensive diagnostic study for designing an intervention plan. This is to be done at organization or institutional level. This chapter is an assessment of the movement that may help leaders to identify and indicate likely areas of action.

The chapter also is an attempt to enable the society to get a 380 degree view of the movement as it stands today. Significant to note that this situation appraisal has been made using the SWOT framework at the movement level. This is different from the SWOT analysis that any organization in the movement may attempt. The elements in the quadrant would vary from organization to organization and from time to time. This chapter provides good indications for action for anyone interested. An actionable table is provided at the end of the book for readers to apply the lessons on to themselves.

INTRODUCTION

Sri Sri Thakur Anukul Chandra's movement, spurred by the prophet's mission, carries multiple points of interface with man and society. Society has its own complex motion that takes care of numerous aspects of human being. For Sri Sri Thakur's movement to have impact on society, the latter (society) was supposed to extend affable reception to the movement. Society should have been more open to the movement than what was experienced. Sri Sri Thakur, like all past prophets, attempted to usher change in the mindset and prevailing social order. The contemporary and convention bound society resisted the attempt to change. That resistance was toned down by 1969 as Sri Sri Thakur prevailed with the provisions and potentials of the ideology. As Sri Sri Thakur went off the scene, his personal charm waned off, the negative socio cultural forces raised their ugly heads to apply counter pressures on the movement. The conventional society could not thwart the movement; instead the former tried to twist the latter. Thereafter process of compromise ensued, whereby a path of least resistance was drawn. Conventional order of the society, camouflaged as convenience and numerous other forms, surfaced and started spreading its tentacles. Phases of moderation in the movement crept in. (Appendix 3)

To assume that that social factors would be favourable for Sri Sri Thakur's movement to have impact on the society may amount to getting into the fallacy of circular reasoning. Reality was that society did not allow a passage to the movement which could have made inroad to the society's bastion of conservatism. Deeply entrenched orthodoxies, fear for uncertainties, inhibitions, passion for perversion, identity crisis of incumbent social role holders, all worked together to dilute Sri Sri Thakur's movement. Sri Sri Thakur's movement faced strong headwinds arising from rest of the society. On the battle front of change, the movement was greeted with terms of negotiation; negotiation to water down the purity, sanctity, novelty of the movement. Sri Sri Thakur's movement as it is today is beset with its own strength and weakness, as brought out in the following SWOT analysis.

The SWOT analysis has been done for the movement as it is observed today from the point of view of society.

STRENGTH OF SRI SRI THAKUR'S MOVEMENT

Sri Sri Thakur's movement is based on a strong ideological framework that fulfils both individual and social needs. The ideology has relevance and resilience to present and future needs of society. The ideology comes as solutions. The ideology in its core values accept diversities, idiosyncrasies and spirit of innovation.

People with assorted background, from different geography, religion, profession and culture, Irrespective of their diverse education, wealth, social status, religious affiliation and all, found the ideology most appropriate to adopt progressive living. Sri Sri Thakur's ideology harbors universal appeal.

Sri Sri Thakur's movement never forced homogeneity and uniformity in external paraphernalia of life. It allowed freedom of choice and preference, while maintaining urge to live, act and grow.

The ideology promotes spiritual living in the household setting. In that sense, it is most appealing to the social conditions. Biological assets of the society is maintained through heredity and compatible marriage system.

The ideology supports science, economic development, technology innovation and everything that goes with progressive approach to life and civilizational upkeep. There are specific tenets for marriage system, education system, and commercial aspects of society, which provide robust reference points.

Sri Sri Thakur's movement deals with social issues of all hues, conventional and modern, while providing solutions to the problems of the age. The ideology thus creates values.

Sri Sri Thakur's ideology attempts to regulate habits and behavior and thereby helps to transform people at large. The ideology can help create refined citizens. Superior social order will be attained by adhering to the ideology and by having allegiance to the Ideal.

Sri Sri Thakur's movement never attempted to jettison tradition. It respected tradition, culture, conventional leaders and systems. It however sought to make the existing systems meaningful. Therefore, the movement created clarity in concepts and sharpened consciousness. Sri Sri Thakur's movement is knowledge based. It encourages testing, experimentation and innovation; therefore, it is scientific, progressive and futuristic.

Sri Sri Thakur's movement does not look at a human being through the prism of religion. All religions are treated alike as long as the principles of the progenitor of the religions are followed in spirit. To the extent, there are distortions in the conventional religions and these have become anachronistic, then one has to follow the principles laid down by the latest prophet.

Sri Sri Thakur's movement now is spread across geographies in many countries. There are energetic and enthusiastic devotees world over who are engaged in extension activities.

WEAKNESS

The movement proliferated under the guidance and inspiration of the living Ideal, Sri Sri Thakur. People got taste of heavenly life, coming in association with him. His personal direction helped to ward off many impending illness, mishaps and disorders from people's lives. Those master strokes and unerring pointers were things of the past when Sri Sri Thakur went off the scene. Then came the indelible vacuum. Leadership, surviving and new, were not seen to be coherent to hold the movement together. They did not do any such thing to keep the movement relevant to the changing society. They did not instill confidence in the society. They perhaps lacked that maturity and outlook as required to provide direction to the humanity.

Sri Sri Thakur's movement is based on adherence to one Ideal. It also requires practice of ideology in daily life by each disciples. The movement expects the participants to follow stringent standards of purity, patience and perseverance. The movement expects everyone to be self-directed; and expectation of that order of self-discipline from every devotee became weakness for a unified movement. Secondly, this kind of adherence and standards, perhaps, got diluted when the devotees' number increased without getting the purity and divinity instilled in them.

Sri Sri Thakur by his ideology and expectation, wanted every individual and groups to be autonomous on the basis of aptitude and choice. Adherence to the principle by a devotee was supposedly a spontaneous growth like a sprout from seed and a flower on the plant. Discipline was a normal phenomenon when devotees follow principles under the obedience to the same Ideal. These kind of self-regulation was instrumental in bringing about integration amongst the mass. On the flip side, a devotee might feel, may be right from his or her view point, that he or she doesn't need any collective association. Thus the high level of individual empowerment made some devotees to remain with themselves, without having any concern for the movement. Secondly, works to be done by the individuals were so much overemphasized that movement failed to see merit in collective initiative and large scale mobilization.

The difference of views at leadership level and divisions in organizations, both led to creation of splintered groups which caused disunity at mass devotees' level.

The movement did not collaborate with other organizations on academic, cultural and social space. Leaders probably felt that this movement had its distinct role and objective with epoch making leadership. They worked hard to strengthen and spread the movement. They did everything possible to mobilize man, money and material to enable the movement create a big-bang effect on the society. They must have zealously guarded the identity of the movement. The movement moved heavy loads with deep sentiment on Sri Sri Thakur. They presumably thought that any collaboration might compromise the core of the movement. That seems to be logical argument to the extent ideological completeness is concerned. That logic however failed to distinguish between ideological framework and social necessity.

Most of the devotees remain satisfied with their devotional affairs. Some active devotees remain engaged in activities like organizing a program, a celebration, a visit, some community work, some mobilization; all of course connected to Sri Sri Thakur. Some devotees are quite knowledgeable persons. They remain connected with Sri Sri Thakur though literary activities like reading, writing and holding discussions. They belong to thought leadership category. There are very few devotees who have rare combination of devotion, knowledge and urge for activities. The movement so far has not offered such major work plan to keep the active devotees engaged with fulfilment. By being active, we mean having urge for action (कर्म), backed by devotion (भक्ति) and guided by knowledge (ज्ञान).

The finance source of the movement happens to spontaneous love offerings of devotees for Sri Sri Thakur. Broadly there are three types to revenue sources for an average establishment in the movement. One, *istabhrity* (ईष्टभৃति), two, *pranaami* (प्रणामी), and three, donations mobilized for specific events and projects. Some organizations also have initiatives like farming, manufacturing pharmaceutical products and book publications etc. Different organizations have finance recourse to different sources. It is not exactly known how much funds the movement generates, as these are closely guarded organizational aspects.

Box 4 - Financial base of Sri Sri Thakur's movement

While on the subject of financial strength and resource capability of Sri Sri Thakur's movement, we may remind ourselves that money has a different utility concept in the affairs of Sri Sri Thakur.

Sri Sri Thakur used to beg (भिक्षा) for meeting his requirement. This is something special in the sense that his begging, may be money or in kind, had different appeal and impact. His tone and style of asking itself reflected that he was seeking a favor. Often it turned out that it was a favor to the person from whom he looked for something. Whoever responded to his seek and offered the alms was blessed. These were not value transactions, but blissful exchanges whose value reflected on life of the donors. Much of these were subjective. There was never any kind of uniform patter in Sri Sri Thakur's manner and purpose of asking.

Every time Sri Sri Thakur asked for something, there must be a purpose to use that item or amount. There was nothing like Sri Sri Thakur's own or his family requirement. He never touched currency note and coin. Nor did he maintain any accounts of his inflow and outgo. His needs were situational, something that arose for somebody or for some purpose. For every donor there must be a recipient. The asking part is known, the giving part mostly remains unknown. Giving part was always plentiful. Both the donor and beneficiary were fulfilled, humbled and earned merit of divine exchange. May be the underlying cause of asking something lies with the donor's wellbeing. His asking turns out to be a way of giving. All these happenings were sights to see, to experience and such incidents were stuffs to unearth the prophet's play for people's wellbeing.

It may be worth recalling that Sri Sri Thakur's mother, most revered Manamohini Devi, used to beg and collect rice and vegetables etc. from nearby areas to run her kitchen (known as *Aanandabazaar* - आनंदबज़ार) that used to feed all the inmates of ashram at Himaitpur.

The active devotees offered some amount in lieu of food to Sri Sri Thakur daily. (*Ishtavrity* - इष्टभृति) Entire amount was used for the devotees' services, ranging from feeding to taking care of someone's adversity and medical aid and building some common facilities etc. Satsang Philanthropy office used to manage that fund.

The resources for Sri Sri Thakur's projects were mostly crowd funded. The devotees begged for Sri Sri Thakur. Sri Sri Thakur's projects generally used to commence with zero fund, nil budget and without detail planning. Whatever was required were arranged at that time; spirit of *karma yogi sanyaasi* (कर्म योगी सन्न्यासी) prevailed. Strangers' and anonymous doors were knocked for alms, help and support, till whatever required for the project were materialized. That was how resources were explored, people were enrolled, projects got materialized and the desired merit earned. The process had all the elements of expedition and discovery. Most of the time, the target was something, but ultimate goal might have been something else. The process, the progress, the path and the promotion, everything was for Sri Sri Thakur's purpose and for people's requirement. That was how the devotees' capacity got enhanced, self-confidence augmented, faith got strengthened, success was tasted, institutions built and services rendered.

Usually at any given time and at a defined place, money has a value in terms of good and services that it can get in exchange. In that sense, money has a face value and it is known and therefore it is fixed in short term. Money however carries a stretched value when it is collected and used for Sri Sri Thakur's work. It depends upon the purity, sanctity and objective for which money is mobilized and utilized. The workers and leaders of Sri Sri Thakur add 'value' to the 'face value' of money by their dedication, steadfastness to overcome challenges and innovation. Money defies its definition of being a 'standard of value', when it is used for Sri Sri Thakur's work.

How much of these spirits and culture the movement can carry forward is left to the leaders. The movement has to mobilize and utilize 4 M's; namely, man, money, materials and management. As the movement does all these, it will be giving renewed push to the mission and object of the movement. The spirit of resource mobilization and utilization need to be carried forward from the earlier years. The type and scale of projects have to be designed for today's time and purpose. Each organization has to deal those issues.

We believe, any philanthropic organization that crowd source funds as sole means of revenue are on shaky ground, unless the organization is very reputed one. Second, all the inflow that come are devotional offerings. Here the donor feels obliged to offer, as per his or her capacity, time and purpose. That attaches high spiritual sanctity to the offerings, but these may not be sustainable from the organization's point of view. Third, free and unconditional flow of funds run the risk of breeding dependencies and lethargy by the recipient organization. Philanthropic organizations must cultivate efficiency and prove accountability. Those qualities will come if the organizations in the movement wear the robe of enterprises and offer goods and service and put their serviceability to test. The organizations in the movement may do well by building their resource base on the basis of the goods and services they render to society. Society is in need of quality products and services.

OPPORTUNITY

There are immense causes of sufferings in the society. Human kind at various strata are looking for relief, solutions, guidance, answers to questions, trigger for innovations, and so many things at concept level, service level, demonstration level and development level. These present opportunities for Sri Sri Thakur's movement to deliver. The movement is in a vantage position to fulfil the basic psycho-spiritual and existential needs of people. What exactly can be done, at what scale, at which place, at what time are subjects that the leaders of the movement have to work on.

There is good opportunity for the movement to play the role of ambassador of Indian and Aryan culture. Inter religious confidence, the way Sri Sri Thakur demonstrated, provides good scope for action. Action could be research, could be some social projects for all communities, creation of awareness building center about life and growth for all communities.

There could be programs exclusively for occupational groups like journalists, teachers, social workers, lawyers, and managers and so on. Each of these would be designed for enriching and promoting the respective profession in line with Sri Sri Thakur's ideology.

Swastyayani estates are to be formed on the line of Sri Sri Thakur's *swastyayani* principles. These estates are to be formed and managed on commercial basis as enunciated by Sri Sri Thakur. The movement has lot to do to demonstrate the process of economic development following entrepreneurship and efficiency. *Swastyayani* funds management may lead to innovative micro financing, cooperative credit societies and some other forms of economic community. These require formal economic, financial and managerial talent with exclusive focus on social needs and movement's vision. Chapter VII dwells further on this.

The movement has opportunity to rinse and renovate the *varnashram* (वर्णाश्रम) system and eugenic based marriage. This is an integral social reform measures that Sri Sri Thakur's ideology envisaged. This has lot to do with social impact of the movement. Objective is that people with superior instincts will born in all strata of the society. This so far has been the most challenging issue that the movement faces. Here the issues fall in the domain of historical baggage, science and choice of future generation.

The movement is fortunate to have endowments by way of personal commitment of devotees. Dedicated devotees are the assets of the movement. Sri Sri Thakur surprisingly made his devotees responsible for some so called global and macro issues. Each devotee of Sri Sri Thakur is enjoined with the responsibility of taking care of surrounding and environment, though these are collective issues.

The movement has to channelize and scale up these individual contributions to impactful level.

THREATS

If the movement becomes increasingly socially irrelevant, then future generations may not see much meaning in practicing Sri Sri Thakur's ideology.

If Sri Sri Thakur's movement only remains confined within the devotees as a religious group, then there is every possibility that the movement will defeat its comprehensive purpose. It will shrink its appeal. It is possible that shorn of its universal appeal, the movement will appeal to those who are god fearing, fatalistic and passive in altruistic activities. In a sense, the movement will be marginalized.

If distortions continue to rule for longer time and gets intensified, then the movement will lose its track and change its colour. The movement has less chance of dying out, but without its liberal and ideal centric approach, the movement may land itself in the hands of unworthy.

The most severe threat to the movement comes from the fast paced changes that are happening in the society. These changes are generally spearheaded by choices provided by technology and revived ethnicity; facilitated by improved quality of living provided by economic development. Sri Sri Thakur's movement continues to address mass existential issues, whereas dominant society is moving towards aspirational issues. Sri Sri Thakur's movement is clinking on tradition and culture; society is moving ahead with adventure and achievement. Movement is churning out maturity and wisdom; social trend is set by freshness and enthusiasm. If movement is not renewing itself, then it will find itself sidetracked sooner before it dawns on the leaders' visibility. It is understood that the task of keeping the movement agile and active is not easy. That however remains the challenge of today and tomorrow.

CHAPTER SUMMARY

Are we content to visualize a travesty of an elephant in chain, on the subject of the chapter? Certainly no! Sri Sri Thakur's movement is out to redeem the mankind from the scourge of inertia and inability. The movement has lot of promises; it has immense strength and abundant opportunities. Threats too are lurking, but only in case of pessimism caused by misplaced idealism. The movement has enough potency to generate faith and hope, which will keep it engaged on its mission of relieving pain and rejoicing divine. The movement is not led by designated leaders alone. Each devotee of Sri Sri Thakur wears a leadership hat. Mass awareness building, setting examples and symbols, adherence to ideology are some key factors to capitalize on strength, seizing opportunities and averting threats.

One needs to give allowance for positive unexpected turn of events in future. But that gives no consolation for the grim reality that might stare the humanity on account of the movement not doing enough now.

VI
REFORMING THE MOVEMENT

Only the prophet is absolute –

the materialized embodiment of all principles,

for he turns all the relatives into the absolute and that absolute is Divine.

– Sri Sri Thakur Anukul Chandra

The Message, Volume 8, page 147, 3rd edition, July 1988

CHAPTER VI

REFORMING THE MOVEMENT

CHAPTER ABSTRACT

Reforms in the realm of Sri Sri Thakur's movement is preconditioned on introspection and ideological adherence. If these two preconditioned are fulfilled, then a compelling situation is created for inspired action at two levels: a) at the level of individual, and b) at the level of leadership. After covering five chapters, we are now venturing to step out of box with a responsibility of shaping the future. There is a surge for action and reaction in the context of challenging possibilities posed by Sri Sri Thakur Anukul Chandra. Sri Sri Thakur's movement has the challenge to take care of the humanity from the point of view of preserving existence, promoting growth and keeping people happy. This chapter consolidates areas of action analyzed and proposed in chapter I to V.

Sri Sri Thakur's movement consists of widely spread out activities. So action for reforms will be scattered and will seldom be unified. There is no central agency so far to formulate and coordinate such reform actions. Reforms will therefore be localized action with *adhoc* span. This chapter outlines action at various levels for the purpose of formulation of plan and dissemination of ideas.

INTRODUCTION

Sri Sri Thakur Anukul Chandra's movement though has elements of eternal and autonomous flow, yet needs leaders and precursors. Torch bearers and forerunners have done yeoman's service to carry the mission and message far and wide. They will keep the movement going forward, passing through generations. The movement also periodically needs to renew itself with updated strategy and keep it relevant through the changing time. That may be a time to reform and auto-rejuvenation. Irrespective of everything else, it is a bounden duty of leaders of Sri Sri Thakur's movement to keep the movement clean and closest to Sri Sri Thakur. In this movement, leadership comes with devotion, dedication and discipline. Leaders play critical role, as while remaining within the core ideological boundaries, they have to be relevant to changing time.

The object of reform agenda is to expedite translating the wishes of Sri Sri Thakur with respect to man and his social affairs. Sri Sri Thakur's movement has to carry out the wishes of Sri Sri Thakur into reality. Towards that end, every disciple of Sri Sri Thakur, the leaders in the movement and the leaders of the society who are currently outside the movement, all together carry the onus. If the target is the humanity, the canvass is the civilization, tools are love and service, then there has to be contribution both at individual level and at collective levels. This chapter would provide some pivot points only, not detailed activities plan.

A leader in Sri Sri Thakur's movement

Like many socio cultural movement, Sri Sri Thakur's movement too runs on the shoulder of some dedicated volunteers. Sri Sri Thakur's movement is largely a socio cultural movement; spirituality embedded. The movement is self-driven as, inherently at existential level, it is linked to individual's urge to propel himself or herself. In that sense, and at the base level, every initiated disciple of Sri Sri Thakur is a 'worker' (कर्मী). At the grass root level, a disciple of Sri Sri Thakur, if consciously practices some promotional activities (*yaajan* – याजन - related), then he or she avows himself or herself as a leader. In that sense, the movement is self-driven, and the incentives comes by way of fulfilment from within. For every worker, the object of his or her drive is self-exaltation and its measure is the pleasure of Sri Sri Thakur, which in some way get expressed as blessings.

The constituent organizations of the movement do maintain formal procedure of appointing their cadre and leader. The one most recognized leadership role is known as *ritwik* (ঋत्विक) (clergyman). A *ritwik* plays the spiritual part of the movement when he 'initiates' (ushers in) a person into Sri Sri Thakur's discipleship. This is a foundational role as the ideology of Sri Sri Thakur is imparted to a person through initiation (दीक्षा). In social sense, initiation amounts to induction of a person into the movement.

It must be clarified here that a discipleship of Sri Sri Thakur does not automatically entail membership of any organization. At the same time, one cannot become an active member of the movement, unless one follows the basic principles of Sri Sri Thakur and the first step for that is to get initiated (ushered) into Sri Sri Thakur's formal discipline. That induction ritual is solemnized by a *ritwik*. Imparting initiation (*diksha* – दीक्षा) is to administer a sacred pledge. It has divine significance for both the *ritwik* and the oblate (the person who gets initiated). More on this subject is dealt in chapter VII.

A *ritwik* is a *ritwik* by Sri Sri Thakur's 'order' and is supposed to play the role exactly as per Sri Sri Thakur's laid down procedure. Here again the sanctity and the seriousness of the process in practice would vary from case to case. However, it must be pointed out that if any distortion, that is deviation from Sri Sri Thakur's laid down principle and procedure, happens at the time of initiation, then it can be inferred that the foundation of the movement is tattered and battered.

In a significant sense, every active *ritwik* is a leader in Sri Sri Thakur's movement. A *ritwik* is anointed by some super leader (usually the chief role holder in that stream of the movement). A *ritwik* is ordained to conduct the initiation process by the 'order' of Sri

Sri Thakur. The 'order' is to be understood in nominal and temporal sense today, when Sri Sri Thakur is no more in physical form. Consecration of *ritwik* is solemnized by following the erstwhile role of Sri Sri Thakur, when he was blessing a *ritwik* with *panza* (पांजा, a kind of credential). The top functionary (head of the organization) is now playing a quasi-divine role which was being done by Sri Sri Thakur himself, when he was in flesh and blood. It must be made explicit here that if some super leader is playing the nominee role of Sri Sri Thakur, he is discharging a sacred role and he must be aware of the sanctity of the role. Here we are outlining the practice being followed in the movement and the spirit of the ideology, without judging any role holder's performance. This must be said that any impurity if allowed to prevail at these level of actions (that is, *ritwik* nomination and offering *panza*), then some disorder may surface somewhere downstream in the movement.

The incentive for working for Sri Sri Thakur is generally self fulfilment. Those who work for the movement whole time are generally dedicated devotee with missionary approach. One thing is certain that there is no regular compensation structure for the leaders in Sri Sri Thakur's movement. The leaders of the movement of course receive some spontaneous offerings by devotees who are conscious of their responsibilities for such pious souls in the society. It is one of the wonders of Sri Sri Thakur's movement that Sri Sri Thakur never made any provision of compensation for the leaders who worked for him and for the movement. He never wanted his devotee workers to take any allowance from the Satsang organization for their livelihood. He wanted them to be gratified on spontaneous love offerings from the people whom they serve. Sri Sri Thakur of course made provision of *ritwikee* (ऋत्विकी). This is a nominal monthly offerings by an oblate to one's *ritwik*. We don't have much idea how the *ritwikee* system is working in the movement through various organizations.

As much as we know, some organizations provide allowances to their fulltime leaders. But that is a kind of alimony that helps to keep the families of the leaders in the organization on subsistence level. Things on the ground could be different at different places. Overall the incentive and compensation structure in the movement is not well defined and it is informal by practice.

THE OVERVIEW OF SRI SRI THAKUR'S MOVEMENT

Sri Sri Thakur's movement does not use man as tool to achieve a mission, whatever that could be. The object of Sri Sri Thakur's movement is the man (woman included). The mission aims at balanced and progressive life in an orderly society. It looks at human life as symphony of body, mind, soul, society and environment. It balances the material, spiritual and social aspects of life. The movement is known for its advocacy for spirituality, and spiritual life is taken as synonymous with ideal (*Guru*) centric life. The movement is pro-science, as it attempts to promote rationality and self-confidence, shorn of superstition and prejudiced view. It is agnostic of conventional religions. It is focused on life and growth and is ideology centric. Here discipline is observed as harmonious bonding, arising out of love for the lord. Honest earning and wealth creation is valued as symbol of efficiency, productivity and service mentality. The movement encourages industrious and innovative enterprises, including small and cottage industries, trade and commerce.

Sri Sri Thakur came for the humanity. His movement ushered an era of transformation through love. His appeal runs across the geographies and religious divides. The leaders currently engaged in the movement must bear this foresight that they are dealing with a force that is very much into the future and for the mankind. Whatever they do will impact the future of mankind. Significantly, Sri Sri Thakur's ideological paradigm touches many aspects of life and living, which are for application and exploration. Unless attempts are made to see those things through on the ground, these will remain only in discourses. Some of those if not tried out may run into the realm of disbelief and oblivion.

Sri Sri Thakur visualized a culture of auto induced service community. In that community everyone will have interest of others in their mind and each will render service to others. It will be self-regulated community. The movement has to have larger and stronger levers of social service and social impact. Society is suffering from deficit of love, trust, care, service, friendship, brotherhood, security, resourcefulness, so on and so forth. There has to be multipronged approach to fill these deficits and cast impression on social system. The social system is complex, being characterized by heterogeneity, disharmony, and disparity, multicultural ethos and so on.

REFORMS SUGGESTED

Presented below are some reforms agenda in suggestive mode at different stages for actions, namely:

a. Knowledge stage

b. Practice stage

c. Affiliation stage

d. Leadership stage

    a. Knowledge stage

Understand and explore Sri Sri Thakur's programs, mission and ideological tenets. Mind the principles that are to be practiced. The core principles are actually few and generic; like *istabhrity* (इष्टभृति), *japa* (जप) and meditation. At a personal level, one has to have abundant clarity about personal interest, goal and aptitude. The ideological framework is to be known and practiced for acquisition and achievement. Care has to be taken for upcoming and becoming of self, overcoming shortcomings. Application of Sri Sri Thakur's ideology on work, on life and in the societal situation earns for you the blessings of Sri Sri Thakur. Blessing is earned by action, backed by devotion and supported by surroundings.

Knowing the chaotic ambience prevailing in spiritual realm in the society, it may be advisable to guard from prevailing trend that might be masquerading as Sri Sri Thakur's views and interest. Some of the social trends in the age of hyperactive media may come as overpowering, but these may be misleading from the self-development point of view. This point of view is particularly applicable to unsuspecting devotees. One has to be choosy while seeking guidance and one has to be guided by Sri Sri Thakur's literature. It is worth bearing fresh in mind that knowledge is light.

The suggested action at knowledge stage is applicable to all the people in the world, including the devotees of Sri Sri Thakur. Knowledge paves the path for right action. Knowledge guards against deviation. Knowledge takes one through gradual building of consciousness and experience. Knowing Sri Sri Thakur and knowing his ideology open the pathway towards practice and practice, in turn, leads to progress. Knowledge is to be backed by action and devotion.

The movement has to provide opportunity for preservation, promotion and cultivation of knowledge regarding Sri Sri Thakur. Sri Sri Thakur's original literature need to be researched on. Original literature of Sri Sri Thakur are mostly in Bengali, which need to be translated to other languages with authenticity.

Centers of learning are to be set up with provisions for research, studies, documentation and demonstration. Targeted, issue based and policy oriented research projects are to be conducted. Collaboration and participation have to be set up with universities and institutes of advanced learning which are working in public space. Libraries, reading rooms, study circles are to be opened. Journals and periodicals in different languages are to be brought out. Scholars on Sri Sri Thakur must participate in seminars, conferences and other knowledge events worldwide.

Opportunities are to be created such that knowledge and expected outcomes are linked to real life, in social setting. Social action groups are to be created who will be linked to academics and research groups.

b. Practice stage

Practice only those aspects of ideology what Sri Sri Thakur wants one to do. It is pertinent to be aware that Sri Sri Thakur has provided a complete ideological package, and that is just enough. It is therefore not necessary to add anything to it, nor to truncate it. It is possible that the package may undergo some corrosion or addition with the passage to time in natural course. However, purity of ideology matters.

Maintaining purity of practice at individual level may require coming out of the shackles of conventional binding and organization's rules, if any. At the same time, association with some organization may be useful. One gets opportunity for group activities through association with organizations. Organizations must therefore be tested for their purity of purpose and adherence to Sri Sri Thakur's ideology.

Keep your fundamental daily practices as per Sri Sri Thakur's prescribed principles. To adopt more than what Sri Sri Thakur said, or different from what Sri Sri Thakur said, may weigh you down because all these could cause bondage, besides taking you time. It is not required to be unduly routine bounded. Keep your willpower and motion aligned with Sri Sri Thakur's desire.

It is possible to derive lot of strength and meaning from the ideology based action. The ideology is power. It has the capacity to generate enough strength, if it is practiced with purity and perseverance. As we do, so will be the tenor of the movement. Collectively, that strength and purpose must be visible on social canvass. That is the leadership's job.

This agenda of practicing the ideology is applicable for both the devotees and leaders amongst devotees.

The movement has to provide provisions for live demonstration of Sri Sri Thakur's ideology in practice. Greater society must get to know Sri Sri Thakur and his ideology. There may be residential retreats where people would live and experience Sri Sri Thakur's ideology approved life pattern. Ashrams (आश्रम) and temples are the readymade places for these practices.

Ideology in practice has demonstration effect. Demonstration essentially means living the ideology in public view. It is not publicity alone. People of significance would judge Sri Sri Thakur's movement from the ideology as demonstrated in the society. There would be demonstration at personal level, at institutional level, at community level, and at society level.

c. Affiliation stage

Affiliate yourself to such groups and persons who really bring out Sri Sri Thakur live for your interest. You need to *a priori* be aware about your interest. You may bear in mind that there has to be a lot of convergence between your interest and Sri Sri Thakur's work plan. This adjustment is the passage for transformation. Affiliation is the means and transformation is the end.

To maintain your affiliation straight, if required, you may have to shed some of the conventional network of relationships, displaying courage to step out to unknown groups, persons and situations. There is no all size fit answer as to whom should one associate with for delivering Sri Sri Thakur's mission. Hence, it is better left to individual discrimination.

This agenda of proper affiliation is applicable for both the devotees and leaders amongst devotees. Allegiance to Sri Sri Thakur is the test of affiliation partner; who may be brothers in faith, or any mentor or may be an organization.

The movement may seek affiliation with outside organizations, national, supranational and subnational stage. Such external affiliations are expected to provide scope and opportunities to work outside the movement.

d. Leadership stage

Those who have assumed leadership role in the interest of Sri Sri Thakur's cause may need to review and reassess their action and impact of their action. It is always important to bear in mind that Sri Sri Thakur continues to remain a live force till date and he will remain so for eternity. No one can escape from the nemesis of what one is doing. Therefore, occasional reflection, self-review and penance may help to clear the cobwebs from the mind of leaders. Taking leadership role for Sri Sri Thakur's cause is indeed a heroic deed. It has divine credential too, which comes with lot of responsibilities.

From social benefit point of view, leaders need to uphold Sri Sri Thakur's unique and incomparable position. Second, they need to implement socially significant projects, schemes and community welfare activities, maintaining the spirit of service and spirituality. People's need would be the compass of such activities and people's 'labour for love' would be the resources;

people's benefit would be the goal. It merits clarification that people's need are not always resource intensive facilities. Needs are psychological, spiritual, existential, recreational, cultural, medical, educational, protection related, and so on. The movement has to be available to people as resource to support diverse needs of people.

Box 5 - Actionable programs for the movement at a glance

Ideology level action

Uphold Sri Sri Thakur. No action would be taken in practice, that too in public, which would compromise Sri Sri Thakur's unique position of *Guru*. He is supreme and no one ought to be placed on the same pedestal where Sri Sri Thakur appears.

By implication that would keep the focus of concentration on Sri Sri Thakur, where it ought to be. Only Sri Sri Thakur's ideology in practice can get benefits to people. That may usher an era of unity and amiability amongst the splintered organizations in the movement. However, organizational unity comes under a different subject; what is being spoken about here is ideological purity.

Cultivate the ideology with purity, intensity and continuity. Let devotees' life be crowned with glory. Let the world come to experience Sri Sri Thakur.

Organization level action

Organizations in the movement have created various power centers and pockets of interest. This study is unable to laydown organization level reform measures. A different kind of diagnostic study and strategy formulation would perhaps let us know that level of action points. This study only expects the top leaders to remain sensitive to larger social reality. Social benefits from Sri Sri Thakur's movement is the focus of this study. World must get Sri Sri Thakur's message in action.

Devotee level action

Every devotee of Sri Sri Thakur is into a world of actions to accomplish and achieve as per his or her aptitude. Detailed work plan for a devotee is not attempted here. Suffice to say that each devotee must cultivate the ideology in letter and spirit, with complete faith and reliance on Sri Sri Thakur. Focused attention, unalloyed love and determined actions are some requirements at devotee level.

Devotees must transcend their implicit barrier and stretch their capacity to success and joy. With Sri Sri Thakur being there, no worries other than accomplishing your work, taking care of health and maintain relationship with surroundings.

Devotees must engage with some such work that would serve the cause of Sri Sri Thakur's movement, while enhancing their skill, using their aptitude and remaining fruitfully engaged with larger society. For this purpose, a devotee may look for affiliation with such association where they would find fulfilment.

CHAPTER SUMMARY

Sri Sri Thakur is the originator of the movement. It is important for us to know that Sri Sri Thakur is not confined in the movement. The movement what we see today is only a tiny fraction of Sri Sri Thakur's mission in action. The movement in no way does represent Sri Sri Thakur's 'to do list'. However, the movement, as torch bearer, has miles to go and lot to deliver. Surpassing and supplanting all conventional isms, Sri Sri Thakur's movement has to lay the contours of existentialism and humanism. For the movement, it is all there in Sri Sri Thakur's legacy. All that is required is dive deep into Sri Sri Thakur's ideology, explore the utilitarian values, and apply the values in the society.

The movement has to carry on translating Sri Sri Thakur's mission to reality. Humanity's future is at the heart of the mission. It is now in our hands to lead the movement. Everyone potentially is a leader in this movement. We believe that this movement is destined for enhancement, excellence and eternity. The outcome of the movement is beautiful life in a wonderful society. To the extent, we are part of the movement; the movement becomes part of our life. Life expands, gets enriched, and meets pools of joy. The movement flows with time and is steered by leaders. Movement will have thriving lease of life by suitable activities by the devotees.

We have reached a stage, where philosophy ends and action begins. We have landed on the endless expanse of perspiration and actualization. Search for spirituality has evolved into pyramids of love. What is at stake is up rise of collective consciousness.

You are a gardener; the flowers blossom on the plants that your hands care. Flowers are nature's creation; these are nature in your garden, close to your reach; part of your life.

Your life is a flower with fragrance of love and divinity.

Sri Sri Thakur is the supreme father; he is in you and with you, work for him and do enjoy his blessings!

VII
GLOSSARY OF SELECT VOCABULARY

He, who knows the existential trail of life and growth with the environmental go, is the leading teacher of mankind.

– Sri Sri Thakur Anukul Chandra

The Message, Volume 2, page 283, 3rd edition, January 1993

CHAPTER VII

GLOSSARY OF SELECT VOCABULARY

The following terminologies and concepts have been explained in this chapter. These have been used in this study with specific meaning. Readers would benefit from the clarity provided here.

- ⅄ Sri Sri Thakur Anukul Chandra and his ashrams (आश्रम)
- ⅄ Movement
- ⅄ Incarnate and prophet
- ⅄ *Aachaarya* (आचार्य)
- ⅄ *Ritwik* (ऋत्विक)
- ⅄ *Swastyayani* (स्वस्तयनी)
- ⅄ Sri Sri Thakur's demise

SRI SRI THAKUR ANUKUL CHANDRA AND HIS ASHRAMS

Sri Sri Thakur was born in 1888 at village Himaitpur in Pabna district, which is currently located in Bangladesh. He migrated to Deoghar in Jharkhand state in 1946 and lived over there till January 1969. The ashrams, which were naturally formed at Himaitpur and later in Deoghar, were settlements of devotees who stayed with Sri Sri Thakur. Lot of activities, including scientific and industrial works, happened at these two places. These were the epicenters of Sri Sri Thakur's movement.

These two ashrams today are home to headquarters of some large organizations which are engaged in promoting Sri Sri Thakur's image and interest. The current ashram at Himaitpur is a new settlement on a land created by Padma River, adjacent to Sri Sri Thakur's original ashram premise, which is currently used as a hospital under Government of Bangladesh. The ashram at Deoghar is home to three organizations, largely led by three sons of Sri Sri Thakur. The Satsang ashram, Deoghar, the abode of Sri Sri Thakur, is under the management of the eldest son. The other two ashrams, are under the management of other two sons.

Besides, there are many ashrams, *vihars*, centers, temples which constitute the physical organizational structure and assets of the movement. These are spread all over India and in some other countries.

All these constitute the physical structure of Sri Sri Thakur's movement.

MOVEMENT

What is considered 'movement' in this book is Sri Sri Thakur Anukul Chandra's movement. It is a social force arising out of the life, activities and ideology of

Sri Sri Thakur Anukul Chandra. In general parlance, it is known as Satsang Movement. However, we have avoided using the word 'satsang movement', as it may get mixed up with the activities and influence of Satsang organizations (bodies and associations). Activities of Satsang organizations are structural streams in Sri Sri Thakur's movement. Sri Sri Thakur's movement has much wider ambit.

Satsang was a concept to denote community of lovers of existence. That concept took an organizational shape in Satsang organization, led by Sri Sri Thakur at Pabna and later at Deoghar. Those two, viz., 'Satsang as organization' and 'satsang as concept' are used interchangeably in general discourse.

In this study therefore, we have used the word 'Sri Sri Thakur's movement'. Satsang associations are organizations in the movement.

INCARNATE AND PROPHET

God's human form is known as incarnate (अवतार). Prophet is also another word for incarnate. There are many such commonly used words in India like तथागत and पुरुषोत्तम which all mean to say the same phenomenon of incarnation. There are successions of incarnates, as God has taken human form and led human life for the benefit of humankind at different times. However, this book is focused on Sri Sri Thakur, as the latest incarnate.

The humanity and society that this book has referred to are of the time from Sri Sri Thakur's birth till now; which means later part of nineteenth century, twentieth century and twenty first (the current) century.

AACHAARYA (आचार्य)

Aachaarya (आचार्य) literally denotes a person who demonstrates virtuous conducts. This study advocates that Sri Sri Thakur Anukul Chandra is the *Aachaarya* (आचार्य) in the movement. He is the demonstrator of the norms and conducts of life. This becomes a misnomer if it is used as prefix to any other person or position in Sri Sri Thakur's movement.

RITWIK

Ritwik (ऋत्विक) imparts *diksha* (दीक्षा). This is in accordance with Sri Sri Thakur's ideological process and practice. For the purpose of imparting *diksha* (दीक्षा), a *ritwik* (ऋत्विक) represents Sri Sri Thakur. Imparting *diksha* (दीक्षा), that is performing the ritual of initiation into Sri Sri Thakur's discipline, is a holy assignment of *ritwik* (ऋत्विक). The sanctity and spiritual significance of the person would of course vary from person (*ritwik*) to person (*ritwik*). From social point of view, *ritwiks* (ऋत्विक) become natural leaders. They become guardian of the family of their oblates. They may develop larger than life personalities, based on their status and influence. These people therefore carry huge responsibility for the social impact of Sri Sri Thakur's movement.

An illustrative diagram in Figure 4 has been presented to show the relationship that a devotee bears with the *ritwik* on the one hand and Sri Sri Thakur, the *Guru,* on the other, in the backdrop of the society, organization and movement.

Figure 4 - Relation among Sri Sri Thakur, Ritwik and Devotee

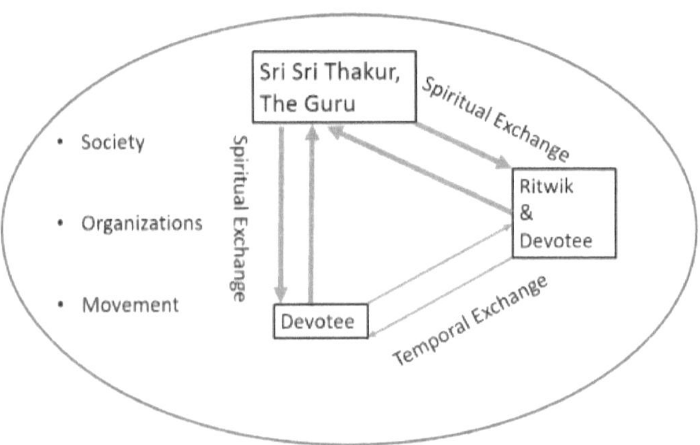

In this illustration, *ritwik* box connotes that a *ritwik* is also devotee. In that sense, *ritwik* bears bidirectional spiritual relationship with Sri Sri Thakur and temporal relationship with the oblate. The oblate-devotee too maintains bidirectional spiritual exchange with Sri Sri Thakur.

SWASTYAYANI (स्वस्तयनी)

Swastyayani (स्वस्तयनी) is a high impact ideological scheme (ब्रत) that some devotees of Sri Sri Thakur practice. It is an advanced deep-layered scheme which only select devotees opt for. It is akin to a lifelong penance, put to practice daily. A justifiable elucidation of *swastyayani vrat* (स्वस्तयनी ब्रत) is outside the scope of this study. It may suffice to say here that a practitioner of *swastyayani vrat* (स्वस्तयनी ब्रत) is a committed devotee with aspiration to scale higher level of pursuit. He or she has pledged for a superior order of spiritual practice, having high intensity of purity in physical, mental and spiritual realm. The practices of *swastyayani* (स्वस्तयनी) scheme requires one to exercise self-regulation and determined action. The scheme is oriented for capacity enhancement.

What is relevant for this study is that *swastyayani* (स्वस्तयनी) has two principles, out of five, which if implemented can have perceptible social and economic impact. One principle enjoins the *swastyayani* (स्वस्तयनी) practitioner to serve the neighbor and surroundings. This principle requires doing well of others; a rigorous altruistic call. Another principle requires the practitioner to offer a sum daily as *swastyayani* (स्वस्तयनी) offering. The amount of offering is left to the capacity and choice of the practitioner.

That offering made daily by reciting *mantra* is kept in cash for thirty days with the practitioner. A small fixed amount out of the total offering on thirtieth day is given to a person who is chosen appropriate for the purpose, as per Sri Sri Thakur's eligibility criteria. Balance amount is saved by the practitioner in his own name in some interest bearing secured saving instrument. Over the years, the saved accumulated offering becomes an investible corpus with the practitioner. That saved amount when gets sizeable is required to be invested in an immovable asset or property that would be yielding revenue. Care has to be taken that the asset or property is well maintained for its value and durability.

Significant to note that *swastyayani* (स्वस्तयनी) asset or property is owned by Sri Sri Thakur and managed by the practitioner as a trustee. This ownership principle brings complex legal and managerial issues to the fore. The ownership of the asset is not envisaged to change hand. This is said to be a decentralized model of economic power in the society and this does make difference to the efficiency in utilization of the asset. These issues require further elucidation, which is not attempted in this study.

Swastyayani (स्वस्तयनी) asset is managed for productive use and the asset is supposed to generate turnover and profit over time. The profit becomes income for the trustee. Large part (four fifth) of the income would be used for people's welfare. One fifth of the profit, if any, can be spent by the trustee (s) for his own purpose. That is how the swastyayani asset or property management becomes a farming or commercial or manufacturing activity and the business continues. Besides, the fresh injection of monthly surplus *swastyayani* fund continues to add to capital recurrently.

At the macro level, the scheme envisages that families and communities will have internal resources for enterprising activities. Everyone would not run for jobs. Further, the scheme would generate funds for community services like education, culture, health and security and so on. Communities will not always look up to government for these provisions. The scheme on softer side envisages promotion of individual qualities and collective wealth. The income from the property or asset will support mental, moral and spiritual nurturing such that individuals become more efficient and productive.

There is a provision that *swastyayani* (स्वस्तयनी) corpus of a group of devotees can be aggregated and a collective asset or property can be created. Collective fund will have the amount to build a scaled up or threshold size asset. Further, when a group of devotees join together, then it helps to manage the asset or business better on partnership basis.

Sum and substance of the scheme is that devotees save everyday by way of *swastyayani* (स्वस्तयनी) offerings to Sri Sri Thakur. That accumulated saving for some time remains in fixed recurring small saving instruments. When the amount becomes large sum, enough to make investment in an income yielding asset, then the accumulated savings gets invested. Then it goes into a typical business model.

Details of the business model would obviously vary from case to case. It would also vary from practitioner to practitioner. At the moment, we visualize a most likely case in which the income from *swastyayani* (स्वस्तयनी) asset will be passive income for individual. However, the provision of pooling of *swastyayani* (स्वस्तयनी) funds can give rise to active business and active income. Collective ownership would make active management possible, at least by some partnering devotees having business acumen and time. All these are matter of details, which one has to outline at the feasibility stage for oneself or a group of *swastyayani* (स्वस्तयनी) practitioners together.

Significant to note that *swastyayani* (स्वस्तयनी) funds create investible funds in the society from the devotees' small savings. That investible funds for some time remains in country's banking system, by way of aggregate surplus. Thereafter, income yielding assets are created, which adds to the productive capital base of the economy. That base, through the management of trustees, generates employment, income to the people who work there, profit to the enterprise, and so on.

An illustrative functioning of *swastyayani* (स्वस्तयनी) scheme offerings in the economy is presented in Figure 5. Household sector provides surplus to deficit financial sector, which in turn creates productive assets in the real economy by way of investment. That assets is used for business that generates goods and services and further surplus and employment.

Figure 5 - Economic Value Creation of *Swastyayani* Scheme

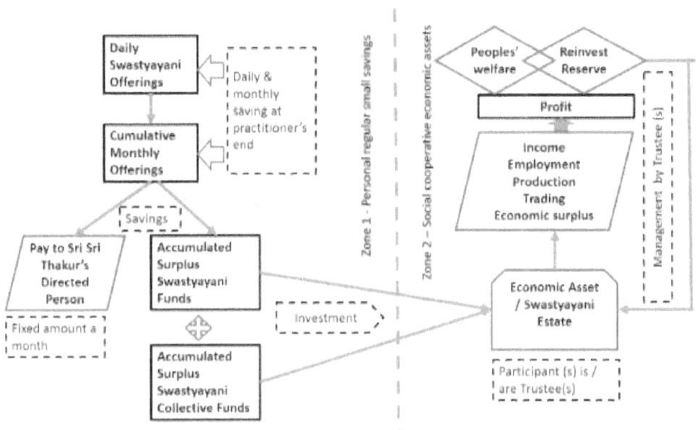

Swastyayani vrat (स्वस्तयनी ब्रत) makes an individual's regular small saving to create collective surplus in the economy, which results in creation of productive asset. That asset when serviced generates employment, income, profit, provides quality goods and services and a chain of economic activities.

Swastyayani (स्वस्तयनी) principle in its aggregate operation represents a socio economic mechanism that creates macro impact from micro surplus. It calls for social cohesion and organized movement. Leaders in the movement have not yet leveraged it to a significant scale and size that can create its intended impact.

SRI SRI THAKUR'S DEMISE

This study at some places has used the captioned words (Sri Sri Thakur's demise) with hesitation.

Chronologically Sri Sri Thakur was born in 1888 and breathed his last in 1969. But we would like to qualify that these milestones like birth, death and in between life cycle phases, may not be taken in the sense these are used for any other person. First, Sri Sri Thakur's impact as a divine force remained even after his physical withdrawal. Second, his was death by will. So we would like to put it as he withdrew himself from the world. For his devotees, Sri Sri Thakur is there, active; but not in physical state.

When Sri Sri Thakur withdrew himself from the world and from his corporeal form, there indeed was a vacuum in the society and for the humanity. That provided scope for leaders in the movement to take charge. His withdrawal therefore created a leadership challenge to maintain continuity of movement with the spirit of ideology.

VIII
LIMITATIONS OF THE STUDY

As a study in exploring an aspect of social reality, this study does not offer conclusive recommendations. The study is an exercise in reality appraisal, knowledge sharing and awareness building. It is an attempt which aims at delivering a mission to the mankind. Significant contextual observations and occasional 'ought to do' commentaries have been made at many places in the study. These are generic in nature; which need to be customized for specific group and in specific context for application.

This study attempted to make sociological impact assessment of the movement. Therefor the spiritual import of the movement has got low focus.

One prime objective of the study is to encourage future research on the subject. Not much of reference to literature has been provided, as the narrations are experiential, which called for less evidence and more realization. Nevertheless, Appendix 1 provides details of 30 books which will impart leads for future research.

The formulation of assessment matrix in Appendix 2 is the original contribution of this study. The value of the index is arrived at by assigning score to 34 questions. Those scores have been awarded by the author. Therefore the index value suffers from subjectivity and personal bias.

References have been made to humanity and civilization. The subject of study covers those mega level domains. However, India happens to be the context of the social assessment done.

The SWOT analysis of Sri Sri Thakur's movement is an original analytical and diagnostic work attempted here. This is time specific and suffers from subjective bias. The analysis however widens the view of the movement for future research.

At some places in the text, though not all over, the adverb used for Sri Sri Thakur has begun with capital letter.

All the diagrams, tables and sketches used in this study are original work intended for illustration and summary presentation. Diagrams are not drawn to scale.

We have restrained ourselves from commenting on the personalities and associations involved in the movement and the dynamics of power play among them, except at limited places where there are contextual reference and need for clarity. We have restricted ourselves to the outcome of the process of past fifty five years, having relevance to ideology, movement and society.

The study has not attempted to factor a force which is known to deeply interact with societal development; that is political power play. Politics certainly is an active factor that shapes the social conditions. This study however assumed that the impact of Sri Sri Thakur's movement on the society remained neutral to politics and power.

Some subjects by 'heading and subheading' have come at more than one place in the book. Contents and facts, however, are fresh everywhere and are non-repetitive. Same subjects have featured at different places in different contexts.

Appendix 4 attempts to understand the perceived low popularity of Sri Sri Thakur Anukul Chandra. These are mere explanations that, in our view, arose as social developments. These are not to be construed as justification for the indifference that Sri Sri Thakur's movement suffered.

APPENDIX 1

LITERARY ARCHIVE OF SRI SRI THAKUR'S MOVEMENT

The autobiographies of Sri Sri Thakur's associates, his contemporary devotees, are wealth of literature to know about the genesis of Sri Sri Thakur's movement. These set of books are a type, exclusive from other books on Sri Sri Thakur's life and ideology. These books provide first hand narration of encounter and association with Sri Sri Thakur under different hard situations. These accounts bring out how the authors have underwent miraculous transformation under the guidance of Sri Sri Thakur and they set out for the mission with mandate from their beloved Thakur. These few books are must read for anyone interested to know the origin and progress of Sri Sri Thakur's movement.

The narrations of these books are in first person and always in conjunction with Sri Sri Thakur. Through these books, one would come to know Sri Sri Thakur from an intimate human angle. Being anecdotal, the live Thakur is found on the pages of these books.

We have attempted to make a list of such autobiographical accounts of Sri Sri Thakur's contemporary devotees, with a view to provide the readers the sources where they should turn to for seeing Sri Sri Thakur's movement in the making.

Table 6 - Bibliography of Autobiography of Sri Sri Thakur's Contemporary Devotees

Author	Title	Publisher	Language	Year
Basu Sushil Chandra	Manas Tirtha Parikarma	Madhusudan Bandopadhya	Bengali	1972
	Manas Tirtha Parikarma	Kishore Bhai Clerk	Gujurati (Translated)	1984
Bhattacharya Guru Prasanna	Tnaar Kathaa	Abhay Dyuti Bhattacharya	Bengali	2007
Bhattacharya Kumar Krishna	Parampremamay	Tapoban Prakashan	Bengali	2006
Bhaumik Bikash Ranjan	Amrut Kahani	Ratna Rekha Devi	Odia	2008
Biswas Ashwini Kumar	Amiya Bani	Satsang Publishing House	Bengali	1921
Chakraborty Manilal	Kata Kathaa Mane Pade	Tapoban Prakashan	Bengali	2008
	Smritir Mala	Tapoban Prakashan	Bengali	2006
Chakraborty Trailokya Nath	Jaajan Pathe (Combined Edition)	Sriprasad Chakraborty	Bengali	1991
Chattopadhyaya	Purner Prangane, Vol I	Smt. Dipti Chatterjee	Bengali	1998
Sanjay Kumar	Purner Prangane, Vol II	Smt. Dipti Chatterjee	Bengali	2003

Das Prafulla Kumar	A Pilgrimage to Memory	Tapoban Prakashan	English	1992
	Smriti Tirthe	Tapoban Prakashan	Bengali	2006
Das Sushil Ranjan	Manar Manish Sri Sri Thakur Anukul Chandra. Vo. I	Smt. Bakul Rani Das	Odia	1977
	Manar Manish Sri Sri Thakur Anukul Chandra. Vo. II	Smt. Bakul Rani Das	Odia	1980
	Maner Manush Sri Sri Thakur Anukul Chandra	Sree Guru Anukulashram	Bengali (Translated)	2010
	Sri Sri Thakur Anukul Chandra – The Man Who Knew My Mind and Loved Me the Most, Vol. I. Translated by Dr. DC Patra	Sree Guru Anukulashram	English (Translated)	2007
	Sri Sri Thakur Anukul Chandra – The Man Who Knew My Mind and Loved Me the Most, Vol. II. Translated by Dr. DC Patra	Institute of Indo-Aryan Studies	English (Translated)	2010
Duttaroy Priyalata	Tomaar Anginaaya	Tapoban Prakashan	Bengali	2008
Fakir Jaylal	Tnar Parash	Aparthiba Roy Chakraborty	Bengali	2007
Goswami Sachidananda	Srimat Acharya Satishchandra Goswami O Satsang Aandolan	Nirmalendu Das	Bengali	1964

Appendix 1

Hauserman Ray	Being and Becoming – A Story of Devotion	Mrs. Audrey Hauserman	English	2008
Mukhopadhyay Devi Prasad	Priya Param	Tapoban Prakashan	Bengali	2004-2005
Mukhopadhyay Janardan	Ke Tumi Biplabi	Mitali Publication (2nd Edition)	Bengali	1967
	Who Thou the Revolutionary? Translated by Ray Hauserman	Satsang Publishing House, (3rd Edition)	English	1956
Nath Umapada (Srinath)	Punya Bhumi Kustiya O Biswaguru Sri Sri Anukulchandra	Charyashram Prakashan	Bengali	2014
Roy Phani Bhusan	Amar Dekha Thakur, Thakur Paribar Ebang Bhaktabrinda	Shandilya Prakashan	Bengali	2013
Sarkar Panchanan	Amar Jibane Sri Sri Thakur	First edition by the author Complete edition by Ritesh Nandan Sarkar	Bengali	1972 2011
	God Reveals Human Evolves Reviewed by Dr. Debesh Patra	e-book by Institute of Indo-Aryan Studies	English	2020
Singh Braj Kishore Narayan	Purushottamer Ashirwad, Vol I	By the author	Hindi	1995
	Purushottamer Ashirwad, Vol II	Vijay Kishore Singh	Hindi	1997
Spencer, E.J	Wait for me, Christ; I'm Coming	Sampa Mukhopadhyaya	English	1985

Truly speaking, none of the above authors has attempted to write about himself or herself. They have written to recall and recount their own experiences about their *Guru*, the beloved Lord. Their own life is the context and Sri Sri Thakur is the subject matter for all of them.

These accounts portray Sri Sri Thakur in his real life and lore. The man-making process of Sri Sri Thakur has been shown at full play in these accounts; hence the dynamics of the movement come out. The authors come from different backgrounds and with different make ups; each one has been guided and moulded by Sri Sri Thakur in peculiar ways. There are events, crisis, situations, personalities, people; with different complexes, different instincts, different nationalities, different occupation, different temperament, different life mission and what not. Each life represents a type and each life has its own story. The books present how the movement has dealt with each one, in different situations and under different conditions and played its universal mission of 'making man', 'fulfilling man', taking each one to his or her peak of accomplishment, overcoming hurdles and obstacles. The accounts are really fabulous, splendid; the play of divine with the devotees. All through these accounts, the live play of Sri Sri Thakur and the formative period of the movement come out lively and lovely. The gracious Thakur is seen in resplendent action through the unfolding accounts. Spirit flying high, fire raging in the belly, each of the devotee authors built monument, which together became the movement.

Interestingly, none of these authors is litterateur of any genre. Exceptions are those who had Masters degree; namely, Sushil Chandra Basu, Panchanan Sarkar, Prafulla Kumar Das, Umapada Nath, Manilal Chakravarty and Phani Bhusan Roy. Debi Prasad Mukhopadhaya joined Sri Sri Thakur after graduation. Braj Kishore Narayan Singh was an advocate and Trailokya Nath Chakraborty was a doctor. Other authors hardly had any formal education, worth speaking. But each of these authors was a devotee *par excellence*; each one acquired high knowledge through intense devotion and frenzied action. Notably, Sri Sri Thakur presented notebook and pen to some of them and induced them to write their unalloyed experience. Sri Sri Thakur heard some of these written accounts and had seen some of the books published. It was an expressed desire of Sri Sri Thakur that the history of the movement needed to be documented.

In the list presented in table 6, there are 21 authors; 32 titles, published during 1921 to 2020. It is possible, some books might be missing here for being beyond my access. Some titles are translated from the original language. These volume of literature constitutes the original literary archives of Sri Sri Thakur's movement.

APPENDIX 2

SOCIAL IMPACT ASSESSMENT OF SRI SRI THAKUR'S MOVEMENT – AN INDEX ANALYSIS

The social impact assessment matrix is designed to assess the impact of Sri Sri Thakur Anukul Chandra's movement on the society. The impact in any social system takes time and there are multiple stages at which impact can be assessed. In this study, the final impact of the action parameters have been observed to make assessment. So, time factor is not considered and impacts at intermediate stages are also not assessed. It is understood that the transmission mechanism of an action in the society is a complex process. Understanding of that mechanism is not in the scope of this study. It is the final outcome impact which have been assessed against action parameters.

Object of this matrix is to deduce impressions about social impact to number. A final number has been worked out which reflects a maze of impressions about the social impact status as on today. The impact is the outcome of actions of Sri Sri Thakur's movement that is observed.

A weighted average index out of 100 is prepared to assess the impact of Sri Sri Thakur's movement on the society.

DESIGN BASIS OF THE INDEX

Parameter

Parameters relevant to the society have been identified. Each parameter constitutes broad actionable area. Action is expected to be taken by Sri Sri Thakur's movement and impact of the action would be on the society. The actual status of the parameter in the societal context has been assessed by their respective score. Each score value is our assessment of the parameter as we observe today against its maximum value. Sum total of the maximum score value is hundred.

Indicator (sub parameter)

Each broad parameter has been evaluated on the basis of some indicators (sub parameter). These indicators in totality reflect the score of the parameter. These indicators are the visible features of the society which get impacted by action. The indicators, in other words, are the sinews of the social parameters. These together are supposed to reflect the social conditions and the situations that prevail. Indicators have been structured in the form of questions in the matrix.

Weight of the parameter

Each parameter has been assigned a weight. The weight reflects the importance and significance of the parameter from the point of view of impact of the movement on the society. Sum of weight of all parameter is hundred.

Difference between Parameter Score and Weight

While the score value represents the status of the indicators (and parameters) today as we observe, the weights bring out the relative significance of the parameter to the society. The weight reflects the importance of the parameter on the society as visualized by the social scientists and Sri Sri Thakur's ideology. While the value of score, both maximum and actual, may vary over time, the weights would more or less remain same. While the scores represent the contemporary status, the weights represent long term significance.

The social impact has been evaluated on the basis of eight broad parameters with separate score and weights as presented in the table 7:

Table 7 - Parameters of Social Impact Assessment of Sri Sri Thakur's Movement

Sr. No.	Parameters	Maximum Score	Weight
1	Internal physical structure of the movement	12.5	10
2	Functioning of the organizations and ideological institutions (cultural practices) representing the movement	12.5	15

3	Social manifestation of the movement	12.5	15
4	Impact of the movement on social systems	12.5	15
5	Universal and extensive reach of the movement	12.5	10
6	Humanitarian delivery of the movement	12.5	10
7	Youthfulness and renewability of the movement	12.5	10
8	Leadership strength of the movement	12.5	15

Each of the theme of the headings (parameter) is drilled down to questions (indicators / sub parameter). The questions are the measuring sticks of the assessment matrix. Thirty four questions have been framed under these eight headings. Each question has been assigned a maximum score and actual score. The score is based on author's own assessment. Author has attempted to assign a fair value; yet from the statistical point of view, that values would implicitly carry author's own bias and ignorance. Table 8 presents the social impact assessment matrix.

Column 3 and 4 in table 8 provide meaning and significance of each question from the point of view of the assessment.

Table 8 - Social Impact Assessment Matrix of Sri Sri Thakur Anukul Chandra's Movement

Sr. No	Assessment Parameter / Indicator	Definition of the Indicator	Significance of the Indicator	Maximum Assessment Value (out of 100)	Assessed Score (out of 100)	Weight (out of 100)	Weighted Score (6X7)
1	2	3	4	5	6	7	8
1	Internal Physical Structure of the Movement			12.5	5	10	50
1.1	The form, nature and structure of the organizational units in the movement	Is the movement well structured, formal, with defined membership, ownership and cadre? Or is it a hybrid variety?	A formal structure with defined cadre is better amenable to discipline and purpose.	2	0.5		

1.2	Level of horizontal integration among the organizational units of the movement	What is the lateral integration level of the organizational units (branches of the same organization and same level branches of other organizations) in the movement?	Lateral integration helps to bring about unity amongst the organizational units, which helps to make the movement effective and energetic. Coordinated strength comes to the movement.	3	1.5	
1.3	Ideologically committed management of the organizational units in the movement	If the organizations are managed well, with commitment to the purpose of the movement?	Well managed organizations serve the intended purpose of the movement well, with positive approach.	3	1	
1.4	Business model of the organizations espousing the movement and their resourcefulness	What is the funding method of the organizations and if the method is sound and ideologically approved?	A well primed, ideologically valid funding method provides vitality and strength to the movement.	4.5	2	

2	Functioning of the Organizations and Ideological Institutions (Cultural Practices) Representing the Movement			12.5	3.5	15	52.5
2.1	Functional institutionalised social service setups being run by the organizations spearheading the movement	If the organizations run social institutions like schools, colleges, hospitals, child care units, disaster shelters, rehabilitation centres, holiday home and the like? If cultural practices like celebrations, festivities upholding ideology and mission are regularly and purposefully held?	Social organizations provide service to people, either freely or with nominal fee, but with compassion and grace. This is related to people's welfare and social security. Cultural events helps to maintain inspirational vibes of the movement in the society.	4	1.5		

2.2	Preservation of Sri Sri Thakur's institutions, systems, practices and tradition	Is the movement keeping the historical works espoused by the founder alive and continuing with single minded focus? Is the movement vibrating with the ethos of the founder?	Keeping Sri Sri Thakur's legacy live and maintaining purity in those practices would help to create and maintain the impact of the movement.	6	1.5		
2.3	Credibility of the organizations and those of the leaders who represent the movement	How much faith and respect people in general hold for the organizations and their leaders?	Credible organizations and leaders are more capable to serve the missions of the movement.	2.5	0.5		
3	**Social Manifestation of the Movement**			12.5	3.5	15	52.5
3.1	Brand value of the movement	If the movement by name and reputation inspire confidence of the people?	Good brand has high likelihood of acceptance and creating impact in the society.	2.5	1		

3.2	Media representation of the movement	What do media portray about the movement? What is the public perception of the movement?	A good media and public perception would go in favour of the movement becoming effective in serving the society.	2	1	
3.3	Contribution to building of socio-cultural infrastructure	If the movement has promoted socio-cultural infrastructure like culture centres, theme park, cultural innovation and renovation centre, health research centre, performing arts and music centre and museum etc.?	Infrastructure for social and cultural aspects of life can only be built by organisations which work for people at society level and which are resourceful. Such infrastructure are public assets of the society.	2	0.5	

3.4	Contribution for making provision for economic wellbeing of the people	If the movement has created such facilities, assets, and enterprises which provide engagements to people and help create income, employment, financial support to people in need?	People look for economic provisions to meet their requirements, particularly in rainy days. Gainful employment of people create loyalty for the movement and movement gets intended outcome.	3	0.5	
3.5	Publications of literature and their circulation, including libraries and public reading rooms	What is the volume and power of the literature created by the movement? What is the readership and circulation of the literature created by the movement? Are there good libraries, websites and broadcast platforms including exclusive media?	Power of literature goes in formation of culture and good circulation and readings enable the movement to keep culture alive and help realise its mission. Exclusive media irrigate the culture in the society.	3	0.5	

4	Impacts of the Movement on Social Systems			12.5	5	15	75
4.1	Movement's impact in bringing about changes in the formal systems that govern the society and country	How much impact the movement has brought about on such social systems as policy, governance, economy, education, law, etc.?	Positive and mindful changes in the socio-political and economic systems help to improve the living condition of people.	1.5	0.5		
4.2	Impact by way of eradication of social evils	How much dent the movement has made on continuing social evils like dogma and superstitions in the collective belief system?	Sri Sri Thakur's movement being science based is supposed to free the society from the hold of traditional baggage.	2.5	0.5		

4.3	Impact on building virtues in public life	How much the movement helped to improve virtues in public life like sanitation, truthfulness, trust and reliability in discharging duty, free from corrupt practices, timely and sincerely delivering public service etc.?	Sri Sri Thakur's movement is expected to improve the quality of life by injecting love and service into habits that spill over from personal to social.	3	1	
4.4	Impact by way of lessening communal friction in the society	How much the movement helped to mitigate age old social disease like communalism?	Communalism is born out of ignorance and intolerance, which Sri Sri Thakur's ideology combated against.	2.5	1	
4.5	Preservation of natural resources and maintaining ecological balance	Has the movement helped to arrest wanton destruction of nature, flora and fauna, bio diversity etc.?	Protection of nature is key to maintain our planet and environment. Sri Sri Thakur never wanted any form of destruction of nature.	3	2	

5	Universal and Extensive Reach of the Movement			12.5	8	10	80
5.1	Openness to people of all nationalities	If membership is restricted to only specific geographies by rule and by practice?	Organizations with open door to all people, irrespective of geographies usually have wider reach.	4	4		
5.2	Global presence of the movement on the ground	If the persons and institutions representing the movement are visible and active around the globe?	Larger presence and activities bring the movement closer to people and enhance the benefit to the society.	2	0.5		
5.3	Unrestricted and universal appeal of the movement	If the movement admits all, irrespective of caste, creed, religion, gender and economic status?	Universal appeal facilitates larger beneficiaries of the movement.	4.5	2.5		
5.4	Ideology based openness and receptivity of the movement	How much open the movement is to diversity and heterogeneity, without forsaking ideology?	A closed movement is likely to have restricted impact.	2	1		

6	Humanitarian Delivery of the Movement		12.5	3.5	10	35
6.1	Sensitive to distressed and deprived people	If the movement has provisions for providing help, support for people affected by natural calamities, public health mishaps and disasters etc.?	People getting relief at the time of distress is a necessary strength of the movement.	5	2	
6.2	Institutional capability to support people at the time of need and distress	How much of institutional help and relief measures the movement is capable of providing? Example; service centres for health, shelters for homeless, etc.?	Institutional arrangements for service and support help people to get relief at critical times.	5	1	
6.3	Care for deprived sections of the society	How much provision the movement has made for the deprived sections of the people? Does the movement discriminate?	Care for the deprived section of the people without discrimination create lasting impact on the society. People get benefited.	2.5	0.5	

7	Youthfulness and Renewability of the Movement			12.5	2.5	10	25
7.1	Youths being attracted into the movement	What is the extent of youth's participation in the movement?	Youths in the movement is symptom of future and longevity of the movement.	4	0.5		
7.2	Adaptability of the movement to disruptions	How adaptable the movement is to disruptions coming in the way? Disruptions could be by way of a new political order, proliferation of cosmopolitanism and isolated living, a hostile group emerging from within the system, change of guard, etc.	Flexibility provides durability and strength to the movement in changed situations.	3	0.5		

7.3	Progressive outlook of the movement	Whether the movement has strength to withstand the counteractive pressure of tradition and orthodoxy?	Movement is unstable if it falls into conventional pattern for the sake of convenience, or to appease entrenched vested interest, or to survive existential crisis.	3	0.5	
7.4	Flexibility and resilience of the movement to variable conditions and circumstances	How much rigidity the movement has picked up so as not to respond to variable situations and circumstances? (It is a negative feature.) The flexibility is more relevant for people who are migrating to different geographies and living conditions.	A flexible movement is more amenable to practices and thus more effective. People find easy to be in a flexible system rather than in a rigid and regimented system.	2.5	1	

8	Leadership Strength of the Movement			12.5	3.5	15	52.5
8.1	Communication and coordination in the movement	If different organizations spearheading the movement cooperate and well linked with each other?	Coordination amongst organizations helps to serve the movement's purpose well.	1.5	0.5		
8.2	Effective leadership	Degree of responsiveness to situations and surroundings and commitment of the leaders to the cause of the movement.	Well responsive and committed leaders serve the purpose of the movement. They keep the movement going with mass participation.	2	0.5		
8.3	Relationship between the leaders and the mass	If the leaders are popular, participatory and the environment is disciplined?	Popular and disciplined leaders lead the mass towards meeting the objective of the movement.	2	1		

8.4	Leadership pipeline is well primed	If leadership qualities are cultivated in the organizations? If leadership has prepared successors, passing through generations?	Continuity of functioning is maintained in the movement, if leadership is internally cultivated and succession is made as per eligibility and competence.	2	0.5		
8.5	Nature of participation by the members of the movement	People's participation is voluntary or directional. If the followers are self-motivated by the ideology?	Motivated and auto inspired mass keep the movement charged and moving. It benefits the people as well as the movement.	3	0.5		
8.6	Sense of belongingness of the members to the movement	If there is dedication by the mass for the cause of the movement and the movement in turn ensures people's wellbeing?	If people feel that they are for the cause of the movement in their own interest, then the movement has high degree of resilience and sustainability.	2	0.5		
	Total			100	34.5	100	422

APPENDIX 3

CONCILIATORY ASSIMILATION THAT HAPPENED

Indian culture and tradition since time immemorial has displayed agile adaptability to change. It is also known for its resilience to disruption. Indian society befriends every new comer and makes him part of its family. Its composite structure has regenerative capacity that has stood the test of time. Indian society treated Sri Sri Thakur Anukul Chandra's movement the same way. Society initially received Sri Sri Thakur with circumspection. Pan India took some time, may be half a century, to recognize Sri Sri Thakur as a *Guru* of significance. It took still more time for acculturation and customization. It did not resist the wonderful and powerful outreach of Sri Sri Thakur's movement. Sri Sri Thakur's movement addressed people's need for solace, relief from sufferings and boost for becoming. People from all strata of society tested and assured themselves about the authenticity of Sri Sri Thakur as a holy man with mission and solution and then made a beeline after Sri Sri Thakur. Sri Sri Thakur's name and image as the latest incarnate soared with every passing year after 1918. All these happened like tidal wave and history was getting scripted in the annals of time, as the God in human form was playing his role on the soil of the earth. People came from all parts of world to Sri Sri Thakur and found their ultimate resort. There was huge turnout of people to avail the live touch of love and liberation that prophet of the era was dispensing. Waves of people poured in and joined Sri Sri Thakur's movement in the early decades of twentieth century, i.e., 1920s and 1930s.

DEVOLUTION LEADS TO DISSOLUTION OF IDEOLOGY

Prophet's descend in the form of incarnate is a natural process of scaling down the essence and edifice of divinity. This scaling down is required to enable humanity to comprehend the infinite and unseen power that God is. When God descends in human form, God limits himself to a shape, size and stature as required for the humanity. A prophet may analogically be understood as a bucket of sea water. The water in the bucket has all the properties of the water in the sea; but it lacks the largeness and ferocity of the sea. While water is contained, it has more utilitarian value and is amenable to handling.

Devotee receives prophet to the limit of his (or her) capability. The prophet is sized down for a devotee to the extent of devotee's capacity; a case of further scale down (2nd stage scaling down). This scaling down is something to do with the devolution of divine to devotee. Divine power at prophet's end is non-depletable. The diminution in the sense of restricted actualization is a phenomenon at receiving end of the devotee. Analogically, it is sun's energy and its impact on the earth. The scattered rays of the sun is as powerful as it is received and processed on the earth, at different places, on varied receptacle.

Prophet's ideology gets delimited when it takes the form of movement. Here dispersion and dissipation take place; a further case of scaling down (3rd stage). Ideology is something given and movement is what is practiced at collective level. The collectivity and universal prevalence scale down the average intensity of ideology. Movement attaches social power to ideology.

When the movement interacts with the society, further scaling down takes place (4th stage). This is a two way complex process. Here one segment of society remain engaged in exchange with a larger segment. Two social segments negotiate, interact, assimilate and exchange with each other. In the process some dilution, diffusion and distillation take place in cultural sphere by way of human and institutional interaction.

At different stages, natural dilution and dispersion occurs. The challenge here is to direct and manage the process of interaction; both at individual level and at group level. The movement of Sri Sri Thakur with its just born purity and divinity accosted the timeless tradition of India with promise to complement. Indian society discovered a refreshing accompaniment, representing modernity oozing out of eternity.

The figure 9 illustrates the four stage dissipation, which is a natural and a kind of compelling process.

Figure 9 - Stage Wise Dissipation of Ideological Fervor

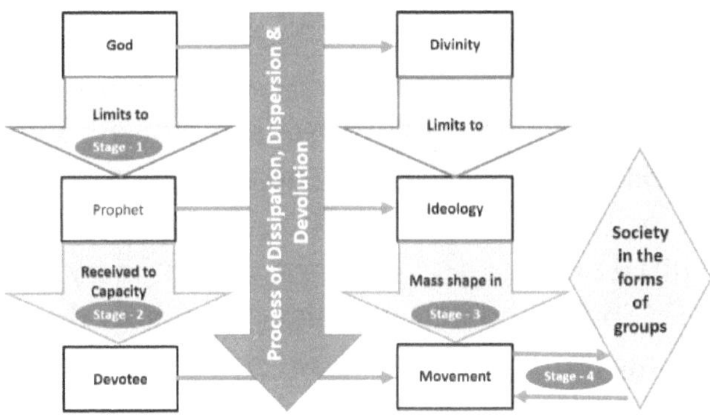

UNIVERSAL ACCEPTANCE WITHOUT DISCIPLINARY SAFEGUARD LOWERED THE AVERAGE QUALITY

Indian culture today accords a prominent place to Sri Sri Thakur as a modern day seer. Society has accorded a place of significance to Sri Sri Thakur. That very acceptance, from our perspective, levelled off the elevated position of god incarnate that Sri Sri Thakur Anukul Chandra enjoyed. Ironically enough, the act of embrace by the traditional Indian culture came with some atrophy which hardly embellished Sri Sri Thakur's movement. The observation is not meant to undermine the great Indian culture's benign tradition to assimilate the best of things from every corner. This observation only attempts to highlight how Sri Sri Thakur's movement engulfed the country's cultural landscape, but in the process shed some of its shining salient features. The movement perhaps unwarily paid some price for becoming inclusive and popular. Its universal appeal and acceptance lowered its threshold of quality in terms of purity, practice and penance.

The movement of course is bestowed with the capability to carry, cleanse and cure the people who join in. It has self-curative power, primarily by way of spiritual practice and penance, regulated by love for Sri Sri Thakur, helped and aided by fellow devotees. The movement always had peers, mentors, and guardians amongst the local communities and in *ashrams* to help and guide the fellow practitioners, who are addressed as 'brothers in faith' (गुरुभाई or गुरूबंधु). There was hardly scope for a recalcitrant disciple, if any, to escape the onslaught of corrective measures unleashed by fellow devotees. When the gate of a movement is open, it is necessary to have measures to coerce people to discipline, if so required. Sri Sri Thakur in his scheme of leadership, had such positions as *ritwik* (ऋत्विक) *yaajak* (याजक) *adhwarju* (अधवर्जू) and *udgaataa* (उदगाता). These positions were kind of grooming ladder for leaders, who were supposed to uphold the spiritual quotient of the movement. It appears, these positions have not been pressed to service to optimum and the value of peer guidance have not been appreciated by the movement. There was pressing need to maintain the air of intense self-discipline. At mass level, these were to be cultivated by various programs. Perhaps, the movement lowered its guard against mischief mongers in the community. The movement's universal reception accorded to freshly enrolled members, without transforming and purifying the inmates adequately, diluted the standards of the movement. Lot more treatment and improvement in the lives of disciples were required.

PASSIVE ACCEPTANCE OF SRI SRI THAKUR BY SOCIETY

Some sections of society could see the divinity in Sri Sri Thakur and surrendered at him by accepting him as *Guru*. Surrendering here created upgraded and refined impact. But large sections of people so far did not surrender and did not follow his ideology, yet counted Sri Sri Thakur as one of the pantheons of godly persons that the country is proud of. Passive acceptance has the danger of leading to imperviousness and sterile outcome.

The movement was designed to wash away pain, anguish and sufferings from the face of society, which was possible by following certain conducts. People who do not go through the process of pursuit, with discipline and dedication, yet swear by the name of Sri Sri Thakur as the incarnate of the age, either pay lip service or play hypocrisy. There must be some very good reasons, either within them or in the society, for their remaining indifferent to active devotion and perseverance. That does neither crown the people with benefit nor the movement with merit.

The slackness in seriousness of *saadhanaa* (साधना) appears to be an acceptable social phenomenon in a heterogeneous society, which is known for its confluence of multiple cultures, religions, followings and ethnicity. Though we justify this as a natural social symptom, still we will not be off the mark to state that this phenomenon of indifference to the prophet of the age by large sections of society is fraught with potential loss. Appendix 4 makes in depth reflection on this as to why more people could not follow Sri Sri Thakur.

DEADWOOD DISCIPLES PULLED DOWN THE WEIGHT OF THE MOVEMENT

Sri Sri Thakur's movement required one to get into the mold of character reformation and up-gradation. Society found it hard to practice the principles of Sri Sri Thakur, as reformation and up-gradation were painstaking exercises. Some sections of the society found it easy to accept *diksha,* (दीक्षा) preferred to be in-club, yet remained dormant disciples. This is natural to expect when the size and strength of disciples expand and admit large slice of mass. For them enrolment to a school of divinity and getting shelter of savior and *Guru* earns a great merit by itself. This class of devotees generally are god fearing people; not necessarily god loving people. Being god fearing is a social virtue in a scenario when the movement remains focused on intensive pursuit of purity and perseverance. But if the movement becomes light hearted and loses its focus, then this class finds room to proliferate. Their value lies in in showing numerical strength of the movement.

That is how, today Sri Sri Thakur's movement has got large mass of devotees with much less load of devotion. These devotees, constituting large numbers as they do, form a segment of the base of the social movement. That has helped Sri Sri Thakur's movement to secure mass recognition in the society. That recognition at the mass level clearly shows that people have come to adore the divine features of Sri Sri Thakur. That mass do display certain level of god consciousness. This base has value for demonstration and this mass become rallying point for other purposes where social weight counts. Qualitatively however, this base is fluid in the sense that they easily get included with other social groups having traditional values of Indian culture. That is how Sri Sri Thakur's movement has got closely integrated with the society and the prevalent culture without having a distinguishing mark on other sections of people who are known for their discriminating choice. 'Mass following' in the movement deterred 'quality following' of Sri Sri Thakur.

MOVEMENT FOUND EASY TO REVERT TO RITUAL AND SYMBOLS

Society found it easy to accept the divine credential of Sri Sri Thakur and started observing rituals that usually go with godly persons. For example, worshipping portrait of Sri Sri Thakur with flower, *bhoga*, incense etc in every house became a usual view. Sri Sri Thakur's statues were also built and got worshipped in temples with rituals. The portraits and statues undoubtedly are symbolic personification of Sri Sri Thakur and worship amounts to rendering service to Sri Sri Thakur. There is nothing terribly off the mark here. The point for reflection here is whether we worship Sri Sri Thakur by our activities or we found easy to render symbolic service only? In the sense of symbolic ritual, Sri Sri Thakur's movement and traditional social practice have come to converge. Objective of this observation is to make act of worship meaningful; to make worship 'worth-ship'. Ritual based worship undoubtedly has its merits. Besides many other positives, act of worship espouses concentration, mental balance and create serene ambience. But all these have to lead to capacity creation, character formation, determination for just action and such other virtues, having impacts on the life.

Sri Sri Thakur's movement takes credit for building innumerable temples across the country. A simple question is why build enormous temple structures for Sri Sri Thakur when he was living under sheds, tents and under simpler roof. Nevertheless, it is acknowledged that temples glitter the movement with impressive social presence. Temples are socially unifying structures that symbolize love, devotion, purity, beauty, divine and sacrifice. Large number of temples must have come at strenuous mobilization, sacrifice and toil. Temples are traditional abode of preserving the Lord and practicing the ideological obeisance. If the temples are maintained as centers of culture, dissemination of ideology, and abode of higher pursuits and dedicated activities, then there will be social benefit. Temples are actually social infrastructure for spiritual practices. Purposeful management will make the temples the true representation of the live movement.

Initiation or *diksha* (दीक्षा) is a one of the ten *sanskaars* (संस्कार) or milestone customs in our tradition. It is considered to be second birth. Sri Sri Thakur's movement makes *diksha* (दीक्षा) a transformative point. *Diksha* (दीक्षा) imparts life principles which are supposed to infuse efficiency. If the principles of *diksha* (दीक्षा) are not cultivated, then it becomes another customary traditional milestone of life. The intent and severity of practice at individual level would tell how *diksha* (दीक्षा) is being treated in the society. This is yet another example as to how both Sri Sri Thakur's practice of *diksha* (दीक्षा) and traditional custom of *diksha* (दीक्षा) converged well. If the desired practice and the intended transformation outcome do not come through, then mass *diksha* (दीक्षा) becomes a sign of compromise.

The movement of course conducts some community practices which help to keep *diksha* live and productive. The leaders in the movement are engaged to keep *diksha* (दीक्षा) living, rolling and yielding practice. Now a days, online *satsangs* are being conducted to help people cultivate the principles of Sri Sri Thakur, even if disciples are not in proximity. We hope, large mass of devotees would come to value *diksha* (दीक्षा) in spirit and earn merit.

POPULARITY MADE THE MOVEMENT EASY GOING

Large popularity of the progenitor of the movement at mass level is generally acknowledged to be a welcome feature for the movement. That is the kind of rousing reception that society has accorded to Sri Sri Thakur's movement in twenty first century. But the movement from the point of view of its original intent and purpose does not credit itself, if people are not benefited in the true sense of the term. Popularity alone is not a measure of the movement's impact on the society; people's wellbeing is. People reap the benefit when they follow Sri Sri Thakur's principles. And following the principles requires convincing and regulating oneself.

Sri Sri Thakur's movement has to trudge on hard path, as there is no shortcut to real solution to burning issues. Broad path has been shown by Sri Sri Thakur, but implementable schemes, initiatives, projects, institutional platforms, all have to be formulated, feasibility to be established, resources to be mobilized, ecosystems to be explored, implementation and execution have to happen, impact assessment has to be done, and so on. Much more than sprint and success, the movement, like marathon, requires sustained pace and intermittent renewal.

MOVEMENT TRAPPED BY REVERSE REFORM

Sri Sri Thakur's movement, consisting of ideology, institutions and practices, was meant to reform the prevalent culture. The exact process of that reform and its dynamics, timeline etc. are not in anybody's comprehension. When Sri Sri Thakur's movement got disproportionately influenced by the prevailing culture and in the process compromised something of its core functionalities and values, then we saw symptoms of reverse reform. The reverse reform process, that is process of assimilation, has come out of our limited observation. May be some are incipient symptoms and transitory. Unless Sri Sri Thakur's movement implements the ideological schemes and puts in place social institutions, operating mechanisms, collaborate with others, there is every possibility of reverse reform grasping the movement.

It may be borne in mind that as far as social dynamics and changes are concerned, there never comes a vacuum. The process of assimilation, influence and infiltration in social practices is a continuous one. Social and cultural exchange is happening all the time. Sri Sri Thakur's movement has to be an active force in the society to create impact.

CHAPTER SUMMARY

Negotiation, assimilation and extension on the trajectory of cultural development are natural to expect in a society. Cultural exchange is an ongoing phenomena. The resultant cultural amalgamation sets the trend for the society, but it is neither uniform nor exactly predictable. The ultimate test of cultural melting pot is people's wellbeing, which is contingent on purity of Sri Sri Thakur's ideology being maintained. We do appreciate that human race is thriving on multiculturalism and ethnic pluralism. Sri Sri Thakur's movement has place for multiple isms. But the movement has to maintain its identity in the sense, the elements of the movement have to be existentially propitious and culturally invigorating. Those elements have to stand out distinctly, on their own merit. It is true that the continuing dominant culture (traditional culture) would like to neutralize the new movement (Sri Sri Thakur's movement), but it is contingent upon the leadership of the movement as to how much strength they build in the movement. The ideology has to drive; and the ideology has to be put to practice the hard way.

We are yet to visualize Sri Sri Thakur's movement on global scale with its impact being felt. The leaders of the movement believe that Sri Sri Thakur's ideology has universal applicability. Quite a good number of foreign disciples do exist and some of them were associated with Sri Sri Thakur at Himaitpur and at Deoghar. The movement has to scale up, speed up and spruce up.

APPENDIX 4

TEN REASONS WHY SRI SRI THAKUR IS NOT POPULAR

POPULARITY IS NOT A MEASURE OF SRI SRI THAKUR'S APPEAL

The question is not about popularity of Sri Sri Thakur. It is all about the mission of Sri Sri Thakur and the direction of his movement. A pertinent question at times crops up, as to how and why Sri Sri Thakur is not so well known in the society as are many god men in today's time?

The underlying belief for the above question is that Sri Sri Thakur was the 'prophet of the age', who descended for the whole humanity. Therefore, his message must reach the humanity, if his descend has to have meaning and his mission is to be fulfilled. It is now hundred thirty seven years after his birth and fifty five years after his demise. What percentage of humanity knows him? Where did his message permeate to? Various nook and corner of the world are getting devastated by poverty, malnutrition, war, accidents, both natural and man-made. People are falling prey to the cruelties of fate, individually and collectively. So called progress on few fronts, accomplished as civilizational milestones, are causing debilitating infliction on some other fronts after sometime. World is looking for balanced development. When people need Sri Sri Thakur the most, is Sri Sri Thakur available for them? A kind of irony is very much palpable; very uneasy reality which we are compromising with.

1. First and most important reason for Sri Sri Thakur's stay in the so called twilight zone is perhaps found in Sri Sri Thakur's own liking and disliking. Sri Sri Thakur was not in favour of his own publicity. He never wanted to proclaim his identify and always wanted to keep himself known as a normal human being. He was seen to invoke the blessing of 'Supreme Father' and treated himself as His messenger. Though the disciples knew him as the incarnate, but people at large were left with ambiguity during his lifetime (till 1969). Faith and devotion on Sri Sri Thakur was left open for testing and validation, which was not easy to do for average people. It was not easy for a flickering and suspicious mind to muster the strength of testing and knowing.

    May we bear in mind that the lifetime of Sri Sri Thakur was actually a period of revelation of the prophet of the age. A prophet's range of efficacy is an age. It is a critical and watershed period when prophet remains active on the earth and during that period he works on multiple fronts and at multiple scales. He knew best how to make the landing and rolling for himself. He set himself the ideal, the exemplar, the demonstrator. So his revelation was a powerful landing without crash. He was like light, which is known for its resplendence; like air which is known for its life nourishing attributes; none of these elements of nature come with any announcement. Sri Sri Thakur accomplished his work of lifetime whatever he wanted to offer to humanity and has gone off the scene. Now it is for the humanity to work on his legacy.

2. Sri Sri Thakur shunned direct exposure to visual media, photography and appearance on public dais. Sri Sri Thakur never addressed a public gathering. He never went places. One of the few places that he visited was Puri, the abode of Lord Jagannath in Odisha. He visited Kolkata a few times. It must also be kept in mind that electronic media did not exist then in India (1888-1969). Even video recording was not there. Having a personal camera was a luxury, which few could afford.

Sri Sri Thakur however wanted his disciples to carry him places and keep him alive for ever, through personal conduct and exemplary behaviour. It is as if, he was the Sun and he wanted his disciples to shine like planets and reflect his light. Therefore, he wanted his popularity to be tested in the light of practical benefits to people. Today Sri Sri Thakur gets carried over through words of mouth, personal touch and propagation by personal contact. His disciples place themselves as spokesperson of their *Guru*. In this process, Sri Sri Thakur's ideology gets tested live. Limitation of this means of propagation is that it is slow; it is contingent upon individual effort and demonstration. Interpersonal relationship and grass root level service delivery are some of the means of Sri Sri Thakur's expression and demonstration. It is a pure relationship thrived propagation, which has its own inertia. But it is enduring and enabling.

3. Sri Sri Thakur did not dress himself in traditional ascetic attire, which normally distinguish holy persons and helps to build people's sentimental view on mass scale. He did not organize any tradition bound hysteric mass *mela* (मेला), *yagnya* (यज्ञ), camp, etc., which would have helped generate mass popularity. He did nothing of the sorts which kind of mesmerize public attention and enchant media.

4. Sri Sri Thakur did not meet people's craving for miracle. He was not there just to grant people's desire to fruition. Today people are crazy for instant gratification for which they flock to places of worship. Some places of worship have acquired distinction for getting devotees' desire fulfilled by miraculous way, which are construed as divine. Sri Sri Thakur, though in a

way fulfilled people's need, was not of a type that he would resort to magic for popularity. He did everything, including magical event, for people's ultimate wellbeing; never with a view to enhance his own fame. He was least concerned for his own name and fame.

5. Knowing Sri Sri Thakur is not just an intellectual exercise. It is not just an exercise in information, education and communication. A person knows Sri Sri Thakur; that would mean that he is following Sri Sri Thakur's ideology, being convinced of the ideological credential. This is a hard job, especially when applied on mass scale.

    Looking at the history of any ideological movement; it is possible to create a cadre; not that easy to have mass following with discipline. Whenever and wherever mass movement has taken place; the ideological rigour has been diluted. The popularity rating of Sri Sri Thakur is actually a measure of transformation that might have taken place in the life of an individual devotee and society at large. That kind of mass transformation follows a revolution and results in evolution. Sri Sri Thakur's impact is to be felt in both thought and action. Sri Sri Thakur works in the sphere of human consciousness that triggers innovation and fulfilment. Therefore, the spread and speed of Sri Sri Thakur's movement is expected to be deep, intimate and involved. It is like a stream of water cutting into rocks, creating a fall that generates power. It is not a flash flood, which catches eyes but creates destruction.

There is a paradoxical reality here. Those who don't believe in valid and meritorious action will not find Sri Sri Thakur attractive for their laxity. Those who are serious in their pursuit and have mind of their own would not surrender at Sri Sri Thakur for their ego. Both the types don't have appetite for masterly guidance for action followed by humility and gratitude. Only those who are 'hungry' and 'foolish', in the words of Steve Jobs, and yet are willing to tread the arduous path of struggle with lead, will see hope in Sri Sri Thakur.

6. Sri Sri Thakur's movement was a kind of war of *satta* (सत्ता) (existence, or soul) against complexes. For every disciple of Sri Sri Thakur, his ideology warrants 'love for the Lord'; active service for the surrounding and a regulated thought and conduct. Therefore, his disciples are subjected to hammering every now and then; of course, they are shaped and sharpened in the process. But the process is painstaking. Had Sri Sri Thakur directed a relatively easy path, would have allowed appeasement of complexes, perhaps there would have been larger followings and popularity rating would have been high. It is only brave hearts who can respond to Sri Sri Thakur's clarion call.

7. Sri Sri Thakur's life span is beginning of an era. His movement awaits unfolding, which is contingent upon lot of favourable conditions. Sri Sri Thakur was ahead of his time. Time and society have to catch up with him. His disciples collectively have to translate his vision and mission into social actions and thereby create conditions in which Sri Sri Thakur's ideology gets demonstrated, nurtured, cultivated, adapted and engulfs the society in successive generations. If the mass disciples fail in doing those, even in parts and degrees, to that extent, Sri Sri Thakur would remain unknown, as society would miss the total benefit of his ideology. If Sri Sri Thakur's mission misses its fruition, the humanity loses an era and civilization faces danger.

8. One such instance of failure has been multiple fractures in the organizational setup in his movement. The Satsang organization, headquarter at Deoghar, which evolved out of Sri Sri Thakur's activities and was supposed to lead the movement, has been a divided house, after Sri Sri Thakur left his mortal frame in 1969. Number of splinter groups are working now, at times at cross purposes, at different places. Activities, socio-economic and cultural, which need organized initiative on large scale, have fallen on the roadside. The leaders of those camps of the movement, in populist and competitive zeal, have narrowed down

the focus of the movement. Most unfortunate fallout of this is that the ideology of Sri Sri Thakur got distorted in its application. It is like corruption getting into administrative system. In the context of this topic, it is to be said that organizations in the movements have failed to undertake large scale resource intensive projects, as a result of which Sri Sri Thakur remains relatively unknown today.

With optimistic fervour, we hope, perhaps the movement is waiting for emergence of some pilot men with fanatic zeal to set the organizational set up on track.

9. Sri Sri Thakur's literature mostly remains in *Bengali*. Many people are not aware that Sri Sri Thakur has bequeathed his ideology through high quality voluminous literature. Not much effort has been made to disseminate the literature, so that it comes to public view. Extensive research work is required for that. Of late, some initiatives have been made to bring the literature in English, Hindi and other regional languages, but those are not adequate to create impact either intellectually or socially.

There has of course been a surge of contents regarding Sri Sri Thakur in the social media during past couple of years. These are symptoms of sporadic attempt to build awareness and expression of creativity. But these are no substitute to efforts to create and disseminate Sri Sri Thakur's literature that contain his ideology and direction. Serious research, massive translation and documentation works are required. Research works are to be commissioned in established research institutes and universities. Exclusive research institutes may be set up to conduct research, demonstrate, deployment and development activities on Sri Sri Thakur's directions, ideology and movement.

10. So far Sri Sri Thakur's movement has mostly remained apolitical. In the context of this subject of study, it is to be said that no political party found it worth, for whatever reason – political or otherwise, to espouse the cause of Sri Sri Thakur. This issue needs a separate exposition. Suffice to say here, Sri Sri Thakur had huge influence on mass; had political philosophy of his own. Given an opportunity, Sri Sri Thakur would have brought the political class to his line of ideology; but he would resist himself to be aligned with any extant political ideology. This has gone adverse so far as his popularity is concerned.

Our observation of Indian political move on the landscape of Sri Sri Thakur's movement is that there have been attempts by political class to collaborate with the movement through normal political process. Politicians of all hues have attempted win over some sections of movement at local levels on local issues of politics. But overall, as a philosophy and as a movement, political class have looked at Sri Sri Thakur's movement with awe and reverence. They found Sri Sri Thakur's image and ideology too integrated to crack. They also have found the integrity of the movement and sentiment of the people for the movement are too pure to be effected by political ambition.

Almost the same thing can be said for today's media. In these days of high profile media blitz, media is observed to take up many popular causes; but the mission of Sri Sri Thakur somehow has failed to attract their engagement. Sri Sri Thakur's movement is a silent current that hardly creates sensational waves for media to capture.

We would like to conclude expecting some researcher in the field of social science to do further work on this topic.

BOOKS ON SRI SRI THAKUR ANUKUL CHANDRA AUTHORED BY DR. DC PATRA

BOOKS AUTHORED

'Sri Sri Thakur Anukul Chandra & Deshbandhu Chitta Ranjan Das', 1992, Sree Guru Anukulashram, Balasore

'Sri Sri Thakur Anukul Chandra – The Man, The Messiah', 1996, Bibek Bitan, Deoghar

'Rolling Existence & its Pivot', 2003, Kruti Dipti Bahini, Mumbai

'Destiny Demystified', 2011, Institute of Indo-Aryan Studies

'Religion in Practice: Then, Now and Hence', 2013, Asmita Prakashan, Mumbai

'Beauty and Bliss', 2016, Charyashram Prakahsan, Bibek Bitan, Satsang, Deoghar

'Vishwaguru Mahotsave 1918 – The Spirit and Significance', 2019, Charyashram Prakashan, Bibek Bitan, Satsang, Deoghar

'In Search of Life: Sri Sri Thakur Shows Light', 2019, Charyashram Prakashan, Bibek Bitan, Satsang, Deoghar

'Life Love and Lift – The Anukul Way', 2020, Mittal Publications, New Delhi

Edited

Proceedings of 'Conference on Indian Culture', held in University of Mumbai in September 2011, edited by Dr. DC Patra and Dr. (Mrs) Meenal Katarnikar, published by Institute of Indo-Aryan Studies

Translation and Review

'A Dialogue on Devotion', 1987, Sree Guru Anukulashram, Balasore; select portions translated and reviewed from *Alochanaa Prasange* (Bengali)

'Sri Sri Thakur & Sri N.C. Chatterji', 1988, Sree Guru Anukulashram, Balasore; select portions translated and reviewed from *Alochanaa Prasange* (Bengali)

'Sri Sri Thakur Anukul Chandra Speaks to Dr. Phani Bhusan Roy', 1992, Sree Guru Anukulashram, Balasore; select portions translated and reviewed from *Alochanaa Prasange* (Bengali)

'Sri Sri Thakur Anukul Chandra: The Man Who Knew My Mind and Loved Me the Most'. Translated from Odia, authored by Sushil Ranjan Das (Vol. I, published in 2007 by Sree Guru Anukulashram; Vol. II, published in 2010 by Institute of Indo-Aryan Studies)

'God Reveals – Human Evolves' – Review and translation of 'Sri Sri Thakur in my Life' (Bengali) by Panchanan Sarkar', 2020, Institute of Indo-Aryan Studies

READER'S EXERCISE AND RESPONSE TABLE

Congratulations dear reader for completing the book. It is now time for you to undertake this small exercise.

Fill up column 'B' in the row that is applicable to you by writing two action points that will positively contribute to Sri Sri Thakur's movement.

Role you perceive for yourself as a:	Two action points you think you will do
A	B
Devotee	
Leader as you feel yourself to be	
Organization functionary	
Participant in the movement	
Well wisher	

You may take photo of this filled page in your mobile and WhatsApp to 9820132213.